# NAVAJO
# POTTERY

# NAVAJO POTTERY

## Traditions & Innovations

General Editor, Jan Musial
Foreword, Clara Lee Tanner
Text, Russell P. Hartman
Photographs, Stephen Trimble

Northland Publishing

COVER: *"Masks of the Nightway," by Lucy McKelvey*
*Fireclouds on pot by Louise Goodman*

FRONTISPIECE: *Navajo potter Faye Tso*

9-91/3.5M/0368

To all the potters who have developed the self-discipline necessary to express their God-given talents and to all the individuals who appreciate those talents.

# CONTENTS

# FOREWORD

ONE OF THE FIRST AIMS of anthropology is to present new data concerning native populations and their activities. *Navajo Pottery: Traditions and Innovations* opens doors that reveal lingering tradition but, more importantly, stress active new directions in this tribal craft. During most of the twentieth century, only a few publications appeared on the subject of coexisting Navajo pottery, for it was dominated by a quiescent traditionalism that limited production to unchanging and basically simple ceremonial pieces. Then, beginning in the early 1960s, these imaginative potters cast tradition to the wind and trod in new directions, developing fresh and exciting techniques and designs, which promise a bright future for this craft.

As director of the Navajo Tribal Museum, Russell P. Hartman has had the enviable and rare chance to witness the development of these innovative trends. He has interviewed many of these potters, and shares with the reader bits of their backgrounds and their current work. Further, he has added to the significance of the modern development by giving a brief history of Navajo pottery production.

Beginnings of change are always of import in the history of tribal groups and their crafts. Not only are they recorded herein, but there are also photographs of these innovators and of their specific pieces of pottery, recording the potters and the changes in their ceramics for posterity.    ix

Commercialization has been an inspiration for this development in Navajo pottery. Too, it has resulted in several good ends for the Navajo: the craft itself has improved, and there has been economic betterment for some of the Indians. Navajos are in need of new ways to supplement their earnings, or even to make a livelihood. Both individuals and families have responded to ceramics as a source of income. As the pottery becomes better, prices rise, and higher prices mean more income to the potter.

Tradition has always been of significance to the ethnologist. This fine example of the breaking of a strong and binding tradition in so short a time, a little over twenty years, tells much of what is happening to these Indians today. It reflects their outside contacts, their need for an outlet for their creativity, of their interest in commercialization, and much more. Herein are reflected the new and experimental stages of a craft after the breaking of a binding tradition. In many ways, there is a reflection here of the broad, general trends in southwestern Indian art as a whole — away from tribal to individual styles.

This is a revitalization of a ceramic style worth watching.

CLARA LEE TANNER

# PREFACE

THE ROAD TO ATTAINING any goal in life often begins with a dream, and that is how this book began. Some ten years ago, when I first became aware that the available literature relating to Navajo pottery was very limited, I began thinking about producing a book that would bring to the public's attention this ancient craft that was undergoing so many changes. Several more years elapsed before my thoughts began to take any concrete form and in that time I became even more convinced that a new book about Navajo pottery was definitely needed.

Once my creative juices finally began to flow, I soon realized that such an undertaking could not be accomplished alone. I needed to identify others who shared my enthusiasm for the craft and who could help to transform my dream into reality. Thus, *Navajo Pottery: Traditions and Innovations* is really the result of the combined efforts and talents of three individuals.

Russell Hartman produced a text that appeals equally to someone with little or no knowledge about Navajo pottery as well as to those who may already be familiar with the craft but who are seeking additional and current information. Stephen Trimble's photographs complement the overall text and especially capture the diversity to be found among the work of contemporary Navajo potters. My own role was to bring together all the elements and players, working with the publisher to insure a unified product. It is our combined hope that this book will lead to further developments in the Navajo pottery tradition and to a greater public appreciation of the potters' products.

Readers are cautioned that the potters whose works are presented herein are but a representative sample of the many individuals currently producing pottery, both for the Navajos' own use and for sale to non-Navajos. These individuals were chosen because we felt their pottery best reflects the range of innovative designs and styles that can now be found in Navajo pottery. Certainly, however, there are many other potters whose works are equally interesting and worthy of collecting.

I wish to express my personal thanks to all of the potters for their patience and kindness, and to the following good friends, who were of much help in extending to me their individual expertise, guidance, and support. I am sincerely grateful to Dr. Patrick Houlihan and Jim Ostler for their competent advice and encouragement; to Ray and Melissa Drolet for a warm place to rest during the days of interviews and photographs; to Susan McDonald, without whose special support and faith in me this project would have been next to impossible to complete; and, finally, to Russ Hartman, whose mutual knowledge of, interest in, and concern for the direction that Navajo pottery is taking allowed us to come together and bring this project to its fruition.

JAN MUSIAL
Flagstaff, Arizona
March 1987

xii

# ACKNOWLEDGMENTS

A S IS TRUE of all books, this one could not have been written without the assistance of many individuals. First and foremost, I would like to extend my greatest appreciation to the many Navajo potters, whose lives and work are the subject of this book, for their willingness and patience in answering numerous questions (many of which they have probably answered countless times for others). A special note of gratitude is also due Stephen Trimble for making repeated trips to the Navajo Reservation, even when this required changes in his very busy schedule, to take the photos included herein. His interest and easy-going nature enabled him to immediately establish a rapport with many of the potters, resulting in excellent photographs of them. Linda Montoya made the black-and-white prints of Stephen Trimble's photographs. Scott Russell of Scottsdale and W. Bruce McGee of Keams Canyon Arts and Crafts are acknowledged for making available Navajo pots from their personal collections. Review of the initial manuscript by Bill Beaver and of later versions by Clara Lee Tanner and H. Diane Wright provided many useful comments and resulted in clarification of many points. Finally, I would like to thank Jan Musial for providing the impetus and on-going support necessary to see this book, a long-time dream of his, through to completion.

RUSSELL P. HARTMAN
Window Rock, Arizona
March 1987

# INTRODUCTION

ALTHOUGH NAVAJO WOMEN have been making pottery for hundreds of years, their products have gone largely unnoticed and unappreciated by the general public, in stark contrast to the international attention given to Pueblo pottery. For centuries Navajo pottery was made primarily for the Navajos' own household needs and for use in certain Navajo ceremonies.

Beginning in the late 1800s, however, trading posts and the railroad afforded the Navajos greater access to Anglo-made containers of glass, crockery, and metal. This, in turn, tremendously lessened the household need for native pottery, and for the next seventy years or more, the tradition was maintained largely in response to continued Navajo ceremonial needs.

This same ceremonialism, however, rigidly controlled Navajo potters in terms of pottery form and design, limiting the range of vessels to standardized jars, bowls, and pipes, and decoration to a simple clay band called a fillet. Even as late as the 1950s and early 1960s, Navajo pottery was crude and generally unattractive. Individual creativity was extemely limited and little or no consideration was given to the aesthetic qualities of pottery.

As the Navajo people have adapted to Anglo-American society, their material culture has also changed, and new markets have been established to insure that traditional arts would not be lost. It was not until the mid-1960s, however, that the many factors necessary to establish and sustain a commercial market for Navajo pottery all came together. With

1

initial encouragement from longtime reservation resident and pottery enthusiast William Beaver, Navajo potters from the Shonto–Cow Springs area began to produce a variety of vessel forms and to experiment with a myriad of decorative motifs. A revitalization movement had begun!

The intervening years, particularly the past decade, have witnessed phenomenal growth and vitality in the field of Navajo pottery, spurred by the steady development of this newly established market and the continued involvement of dealer-collectors. A select group of potters has responded with an ever greater variety of vessel forms and designs, as well as with greater attention to overall quality. Other potters have introduced painted wares depicting Navajo motifs not previously used on pottery.

The market for Navajo pottery is still in a state of growth and exciting change. The number of potters is increasing as the market steadily expands. Production continues to be centered in the Shonto–Cow Springs area of the Navajo Reservation, but even outside that area, many other potters produce wares both for sale to non-Navajos and for traditional Navajo use.

Navajo pottery can now be found in many craft shops, galleries, and museum gift shops both on and around the Navajo Reservation, as well as in major cities throughout the Southwest and West. Collectors, decorators, and the general public have come to appreciate more and more the simplicity of Navajo pitch-coated pottery and, most recently, the newer painted varieties. Predictably, the cost of Navajo pottery has steadily increased over the past decade, but overall, it is still considerably less expensive than comparable Pueblo wares.

The following chapters will review the history of the Navajo pottery tradition and then examine the events and factors that contributed to its decline and subsequent revitalization. Finally, the lives and works of a select group of contemporary Navajo potters will be discussed, highlighting the finest Navajo pottery being made today.

# CHAPTER 1

# THE NAVAJO PEOPLE: A HISTORICAL OVERVIEW

AMONG PRESENT–DAY Indian tribes recognized by the U. S. federal government, the Navajos constitute the largest tribe, with a population approaching 200,000 individuals and a land base covering portions of Arizona, New Mexico, and Utah. In their native language, the Navajos call themselves "Diné," meaning "the people."

It is generally thought that the Navajos migrated southward from the region that today encompasses Canada, along with other Athabaskan speakers, into northcentral New Mexico as early as 1300–1400, and settled in an area known today as "Dinétah," an area of high mesas and deep canyons comprising the upper drainages of the San Juan River. Early Navajo sites can be found throughout Gobernador and Largo canyons and other San Juan River tributaries. There, the early Navajo people gradually adopted an agricultural lifestyle, supplementing their crops of corn and squash by hunting and gathering.

Social organization can only be inferred from sparse archaeological data or extrapolated from known social patterns of later periods, but it seems probable that throughout the Dinétah Period (ca. 1500–1700), the Navajos lived in independent extended family groups. Leadership may have been centered among men known as headmen, who were chosen on the basis of their leadership qualities and were responsible only for the people living in a certain area or for one or more extended family groups. Except for a shared language and other cultural traits and occasional group cooperation for hunting or defensive purposes, there probably was no sense of political or tribal identity during this time.

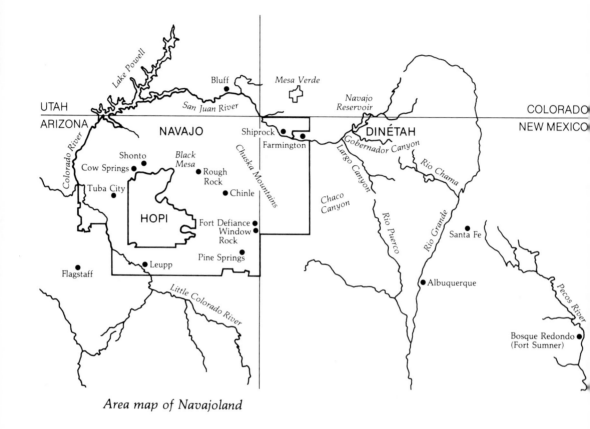

*Area map of Navajoland*

As the Navajos adapted to their homeland, contact with other groups was inevitable. History has recorded many instances of hostility between the Navajos and the Utes. Indeed, it was the Ute presence, more than any other factor, that probably set the northern boundary of Navajo occupation and may have been responsible, in part, for the eventual Navajo abandonment of the Dinétah area (Schroeder 1965:59; Reeve 1960:202–4).

Navajo-Pueblo relations were more varied. Trade between the two groups became a part of the region's economy, and from the Pueblo people, the Navajos adopted many cultural traits. Portions of Navajo ceremonialism, for example, are closely related to Pueblo practices and beliefs, and even Navajo dress gradually took on more and more puebloan characteristics, especially after the Navajo adopted puebloan weaving

4

technology. Agricultural methods also appear to have been borrowed and modified by the Navajos.

The coming of the Spanish had profound effects upon the Navajos, although contact between the two was not always of a direct nature. Living on the frontier of Spanish influence, the Navajos, unlike the Puebloans, were regarded by the Spaniards, at least initially, neither as a source of economic capital nor as a pool of potential Christian converts, although several futile attempts were made to establish missions among the Navajos. Rather, Spanish influence was of a more indirect nature.

The Spanish brought horses with them and eventually these came into the hands of the Navajos. The impact was both profound and lasting. Horses made greater mobility possible not only for the Navajos, but also for their enemies, the Utes, thus opening the way for raiding and counter-raiding.

As the Spanish took control of the Southwest, they exacted tribute from their subjects in the form of manufactured goods and agricultural products. When Spanish domination became more than the Pueblo people could bear, they successfully united and drove the Spanish out of New Mexico in 1680. Pueblo independence, however, was short-lived. In 1692, Spanish rule was reestablished, and fearing Spanish reprisals for their role in the successful 1680 revolt, members of certain northern pueblos, particularly Jemez Pueblo, fled westward and took refuge among the Navajos in the late seventeenth and early eighteenth centuries (Forbes 1960: 270–72). This Navajo-Pueblo union is documented at numerous sites in Dinétah that include clusters of hogans and pueblolike structures, along with painted pottery and other crosscultural manifestations (Carlson 1965; Kidder 1922).

Along with their horses, the Spanish also brought sheep. The Dinétah's rough terrain, however, was poorly suited to sheep herding. Consequently, herding was of little economic importance to the Navajos until the latter half of the 1700s. By then, decades of Ute and Comanche attacks had forced the Navajos to move farther to the southwest into present-day Arizona, and as they did so, they acquired more and more sheep. Larger grazing areas were continually sought, sometimes necessitating additional population shifts. Quick to adopt the upright Pueblo loom and weaving techniques, Navajo women soon excelled at their craft. Navajo textiles were traded throughout the Southwest and among the Plains tribes, among whom fine Navajo Chief blankets became status symbols.

Increasing encroachment into eastern Navajo territory by Spanish settlers during the second half of the 1700s resulted in intermittent clashes with the Navajos, followed by brief periods of uneasy calm. In 1821 when Mexico won its independence from Spain, present-day New Mexico and its inhabitants came under Mexican rule. Under the new government, the practice of Indian slavery reached its highest levels and the Navajos became the primary target for those who supplied captive slaves (Brugge 1983:495).

The Mexican Period ended in 1846 when the northern frontier was ceded to the United States. With America's subsequent westward expansion, the number of conflicts between Navajos and ranchers in New Mexico greatly increased. Between 1805 and 1861, no fewer than thirteen separate treaties were signed between the Navajos and Mexico or the United States (Brugge and Correll 1971). None of these treaties lasted, however, because neither the Mexicans nor the Americans understood Navajo social organization, still based upon the system of headmen. A treaty signed by one or even by several Navajo headmen in no way obligated those who had not agreed to it. This simple fact went unrecognized for decades and led to repeated charges of treaty violations and renewed conflicts.

By the 1860s, the situation bordered on open warfare, and in a feigned attempt to resolve the issue once and for all in favor of the settlers (see Thompson 1976 and Bailey 1970 for other possible motives on the part of the government), George Carleton persuaded federal officials to remove the Navajos (and southern Apaches) to Fort Sumner, newly established along the Pecos River in eastern New Mexico. During the winter of 1863–64, approximately eight thousand Navajos surrendered in the face of starvation and were subsequently force-marched to Fort Sumner. There, they cleared huge tracts of land for agricultural fields and dug irrigation canals.

The Navajos endured the conditions at Fort Sumner for more than four years, but an unstable water supply, a rapid depletion of firewood, repeated crop failure, widespread disease and death, military graft and corruption, continued Comanche raiding against the settlement, and staggering costs finally forced government officials to close the fort in 1868. The Treaty of 1868, signed at Fort Sumner by all the Navajo headmen present, set aside a small portion of the former Navajo homeland as the Navajo Indian Reservation, and it was there that the surviving Navajos returned. Each returning family was issued provisions, and additional rations were issued in the years immediately following the return from what remains one of the most bitter episodes of Navajo history. The Treaty of 1868 is still the basis for present-day relations between the Navajo Nation and the federal government.

In the decades following their return, the Navajos became increasingly familiar with a new institution, the trading post. With the opening of each new post, the Navajos gained access to an ever-growing number of non-native goods, and throughout the remote reservation, trading posts became social centers where Navajos met each other and exchanged information and news. Early traders were the only people fluent in both English and Navajo, and so they served as liaisons between the government and the Navajo people. Their skills as doctors, lawyers, undertakers, postmen, and general peacekeepers were also frequently called upon.

Until the 1920s the Navajo people continued to be guided by a number of respected headmen who reported independently to a government-appointed agent. Under this system, the Navajos still had no real political unity, and issues were decided only in terms of their effects upon the residents of a certain portion of the reservation. Matters changed, however, in the early 1920s when oil was discovered in the northern portion of the reservation. Some Navajos favored developing the oil fields for the exclusive benefit of the northern reservation residents; others argued that the resources belonged to all Navajo people and that any benefits should be shared equally. As a result, a council of tribal leaders was set up for the sole purpose of deciding how energy resources would be developed.

The 1930s mark another bitter period in Navajo history. By that time, Navajo sheep and livestock greatly exceeded the land's carrying capacity, causing severe soil erosion. To deal with the problem, the government instituted a policy of stock reduction. The need for such a program, in order to improve the overall Navajo economy, cannot be denied, but the methods by which it was carried out were less than fair. Individuals with small holdings were especially hurt, and the scenes of horses and sheep, shot and left to rot, both angered and confused Navajos (U.S. Congress 1937:17988; Roessel and Johnson 1974:162).

The decades since the 1930s have seen the Navajo population increase

7

dramatically, as tribal leaders wrestle with the problems of ushering a people into the modern world while still maintaining their traditional culture. Today the Navajo people are governed by a Tribal Council of eighty-eight representatives, chosen from more than one hundred local units of government known as chapters. Each representative, as well as the presiding chairman and vice-chairman, is elected for a four-year term.

Like people in many other parts of the world, the Navajos are not always able to control political and economic conditions and events that might ultimately affect them. More and more Navajos are moving into reservation towns to be closer to their jobs, while pastoral activities decline as the competition for grazing land becomes ever greater, brought about by population growth, withdrawal of lands for community needs, and economic development including strip mining and other energy-related activities.

All of these have an impact upon traditional Navajo life and place additional strains upon family relationships. Elders may no longer have the security of having their children and grandchildren nearby, and without their grandparents, young children may not learn traditional values as they grow up. Even the Navajo language is threatened as more families move to towns and cities. Clearly, education and economic development have their own price tags, and it is a difficult decision indeed for tribal leaders to decide just how high a price the Navajo Nation can afford to pay.

# CHAPTER 2

# NAVAJO POTTERY: A CULTURAL AND SOCIAL PERSPECTIVE

**L**IKE SO MANY ITEMS within Navajo material culture, the real importance of pottery lies not so much in its functional or utilitarian uses, but rather in its place within the overall cultural framework. According to Navajo belief, pottery making was one of the crafts given by the Holy People even before the Diné emerged into the present world. Its special significance is preserved in the oral history and in ceremonial texts and songs that make frequent references to pottery.

In one version of the Navajo Creation Story recorded by Washington Matthews (1897:70), hermaphrodite twins born to First Man and First Woman were assigned the task of guarding a dam and irrigation ditches against attack by Pueblo people. While keeping watch, the one guarding the dam fashioned first a plate, then a bowl and a dipper, while the other made a wicker water bottle.

Additional references to pottery and its prescribed uses can be found in those portions of the oral history relating to specific ceremonies, particularly Blessingway (Wyman 1970:117) and Enemy Way (Haile 1938:215, 217, 263). These brief passages relate how pottery first came to be used in the particular ceremony and how it is to be used each time the ceremony is performed. Numerous anthropological studies of Navajo ceremonialism, mythology, and philosophy have been published over the years, but perhaps an even greater volume of Navajo ceremonial knowledge has never been written down (in accordance with Navajo wishes) and continues to be transmitted orally by a medicine man to his apprentice(s) over a period of many years. Suffice it to say that pottery has an ancient and respected place within Navajo teachings.

When Navajo people, particularly potters, look at a finished pot, they see much more than the physical object to be used as a container. Rather, a pot embodies familial relationships and responsibilities, age-old traditions concerning the proper way of making a pot, strong ties to Mother Earth, and a host of other principles that have been handed down from one generation of potters to another over the course of several centuries. Many of these principles and thoughts defy being written down, but they are, nevertheless, ever present in the potter's mind, albeit sometimes unconsciously.

Because western values are much more object oriented than are those of Navajo society, it may seem odd that so little emphasis is apparently placed upon the finished product. Nevertheless, the Navajo often attribute far greater significance to the thoughts and processes involved in making an object than they do to the object itself. The embodied traditions and values are paramount, and, as we shall see in a later chapter, these principles have helped to maintain traditions such as pottery making and weaving, even when the domestic utilitarian needs for such items have ceased to exist within the tribe. Only with the increasing commercialization of some traditional crafts has the importance of the finished product sometimes begun to overshadow the underlying cultural principles.

The most important unit in Navajo society is the family. Familial responsibilities are all-important, and pottery making affords many opportunities to reinforce ties between generations, allowing many family members to participate in the overall pottery tradition. Gathering the materials necessary for pottery making is the first step in which various family members might help. The dense clay is heavy and often requires a man's strength to remove it from its natural deposits. Later, even children can assist in grinding and cleaning it, preparatory to its actual use. The same is true of collecting and processing tempering materials and piñon pitch.

The act of making the pottery presents additional opportunities for strengthening family ties. In earlier times, potters usually worked in isolation from other family members, but occasionally, young girls were allowed to observe their grandmothers or mothers at work and were urged to follow their examples. Pottery-making skills are still handed down within families, but many of today's potters have learned from relatives other than their grandmothers or mothers.

The relationship between teacher and student is very important in Navajo society and should not be overlooked. In the past, the relationship with one's grandparents was especially significant in preserving the Navajo language, group values, and other traditions such as weaving. Before most children attended daily schools and lived in towns, they spent long periods at home with their grandparents, who would relate traditional Navajo stories, instruct them in their native language, and teach them Navajo ways and traditions. As we shall see in a later chapter, the breakdown of this teacher-student relationship may have been one of several factors contributing to the decline in Navajo pottery production beginning in the late 1800s.

Once a pottery vessel has been made, polishing, firing, and applying a coat of pitch are other steps that are now sometimes shared by family members. In the course of these activities, an elder member of the family might further relate stories from the oral history that tell about the significance of each step. Also, by involving themselves in the various stages of pottery making, younger members of the family gradually learn the proper way of making pots.

Although the shapes and designs of pottery are largely determined by intended use, they also relate to group identity. The vessel forms and designs traditionally used by Navajo potters were, in a sense, very real symbols of tribal identity. Much of the pottery being made today, although obviously different in many respects from that which was made twenty or more years ago, still maintains the tradition of unpainted pitch-coated wares, decorated more often than not with a clay band around the neck, clearly identifying it as Navajo.

The importance of Navajo pottery in a social context must not be viewed solely in terms of group behavior and beliefs, however. Historically, pottery has had two primary uses within Navajo society; it is only recently that these uses have been overshadowed to some extent by commercial considerations.

First, pottery served a very real domestic need in Navajo households, each of which maintained a limited inventory of jars, bowls, dippers, and canteens for the storage and preparation of food. The need to store large

*Navajo pottery drum (Navajo Tribal Museum collection)*

quantities of foodstuffs for long periods required the production of very large jars such as those found on many early Navajo sites. It was not until the Navajo began abandoning the Dinétah area and increasingly adopted a sheep-herding economy in the latter half of the eighteenth century, becoming more mobile in the process, that pots became smaller in size and more portable. The second use for pottery by the Navajos was in a ceremonial context. A number of Navajo ceremonies require the use of Navajo-made pottery for certain ritual functions. Jars for ritual cooking and for fashioning into drums, bowls for ceremonial cleansings and for the storage of dry pigments and other materials by the medicine man, and smoking pipes are the principal vessel forms used ceremonially. These continue to be in widespread demand by Navajos and are sometimes passed down in families as treasured heirlooms.

The principal Navajo ceremony requiring Navajo pottery is that of Enemy Way, performed frequently throughout the summer months. Intended to rid a Navajo of the ghosts of an enemy, this ceremony is invoked today to protect an individual from all sorts of harmful agents, the definition of "enemy" being very broad. Also known as a "Squaw Dance," Enemy Way attracts large crowds for the accompanying social dances, which utilize a drum fashioned from a pottery jar and fitted with a skin covering. The covering is fastened to the accompaniment of specialized songs, and to improve the drum's tonal qualities, a small amount of water

*Navajo pottery pipes (Collection of Jan Musial)*

is placed inside the jar. Only men are permitted to play these drums, and once a jar has been so used, it may never be used for cooking.

More central to the actual Enemy Way ceremony, ritually prescribed food is prepared in a specially chosen pottery jar and served to the "patient." No sandpaintings are created as part of Enemy Way, but in other ceremonies a medicine man might use small bowls to keep various colored dry pigments and other paraphernalia.

Smoking is also a part of many Navajo rituals and is used to initiate other nonritual activities such as hunting. To serve these needs, the Navajo make a variety of pottery pipes. These may be made by both men and women and some are even designated "male" or "female" with the placement of small bits of turquoise or white shell, respectively, on the exterior of the pipe's bowl. Tschopik (1941:55–65) offers a detailed discussion of the various pipe forms and specific circumstances relating to their manufacture and use.

## CHAPTER 3

# NAVAJO POTTERY TECHNOLOGY

TRADITIONAL NAVAJO pottery making requires few materials and equally few tools. Clay mixed with water and a tempering material, such as ground pottery sherds, sand, or volcanic cinders, is shaped and processed by hand. Corncobs, sticks, gourd scrapers, and a few polishing stones are standard tools. Even elaborate decorating may require a tool fashioned from something as simple as the pull tab from a soda can. After a pot is fired, a coating of piñon pitch is applied to it with a rag-wrapped stick.

The most important ingredient of pottery is, of course, the clay. Although clay deposits can be found in many locations across the Navajo Reservation, only certain types are used for pottery making. Each potter has his or her preferred clay source, but the most abundant deposits are located in the Shonto–Cow Springs region and on Black Mesa. Learning which clay is suitable, and which is not, can be a matter of trial and error, but the experienced potter can often determine this solely on the basis of the clay's texture, color, or smell.

Some potters report that certain clays are better suited for large pots and others for small pots. Also, depending upon the specific mineral content, different clays will yield different colors when fired. For these reasons, it is not uncommon for a potter to gather clay from more than one location, depending upon the size of the pot to be made and/or the desired color.

Because of the dense nature of clay, it is sometimes necessary to use an axe to literally chop blocks of it from the natural deposit. Once collected,

*Raw clay drying*

the clay is broken into smaller pieces and soaked thoroughly to make it more manageable. After it has again dried, the clay is finely ground, and small pebbles and other debris, such as sticks, are picked out. As a final measure, the ground clay might also be sifted through a fine-meshed screen.

Once ground and cleaned, the clay is mixed with water and sand, volcanic cinders, or broken pieces of pottery that have been gathered at prehistoric sites found throughout the region. These tempering materials have also been pulverized beforehand and are added to the clay to help bind the clay particles together. The choice of which material to use as temper is largely a matter of personal preference, experience, and/or belief, but each does produce slightly different results. The majority of potters use crushed pottery sherds because the irregular shapes of the ground pottery pieces can best bind the clay particles together. Other potters use volcanic cinders. This material is more difficult to process, but those who use it claim that it produces stronger pots. Sand is the least preferred tempering material, probably because the relative uniformity in both shape and size of sand grains lessens its ability to hold the clay particles together. A very few potters who claim not to use any tempering material at all may actually mix together several types of clay, thereby utilizing tempering particles naturally present in the clay and maximizing the binding qualities of each type.

The ratio of clay to temper is also a matter of personal preference and experience, determined by the feel of the clay and its color. If too much temper is added, the clay will be crumbly. On the other hand, if too little is added, the newly formed vessel will crack while drying. Once the proper mix of clay and temper is attained, more water is added and all are thoroughly mixed. At this stage, some potters prefer to let the "paste" rest, or "cure," for a few days, while others may use it immediately.

The first step in forming a vessel is to shape the base. For this, a small ball of clay is flattened like a pancake and the edges are gradually turned upward to form the beginnings of the vessel's walls. This may be done entirely freehand or in the base of a broken vessel similar in size to the one being made. A few of today's potters also use stainless steel bowls or plastic margarine tubs to insure that the pot bases are of uniform shape and thickness.

When the base is completed and dry enough to support additional weight without collapsing, a small amount of clay is rolled out into a snakelike coil. Depending on the size of the vessel to be made, the coil will be between one-quarter and one-half inch thick. The upper edge of the base is moistened with water and the clay coil is then laid on top. When one revolution is completed, the coil is pinched off and the ends are joined together. Several coils may be added in this manner before they are scraped smooth on the inside and the outside, usually with a corncob. As the pot grows in height, the potter constantly turns it to insure a uniform shape and thickness. Before each new coil is added, the previous coil is moistened to insure that the two will stick together. For this purpose, a bowl of water is always near at hand, and the potter constantly dips his or her hands into it.

Once the vessel has reached the desired shape and size, the interior and exterior surfaces may again be scraped with a piece of gourd or pottery and lightly polished. This further binds the clay particles together and smooths out any surface irregularities that may have gone unnoticed during the coiling process. In earlier times, this final surface treatment was ac-

a

*Navajo pottery-making techniques:*
*a) patting out base for a Navajo*
*wedding vase, b,c) adding coil to the*
*vase, d) forming the vase, e) shaping*
*the vase. Betty Manygoats pictured.*

b

c

18

d

e

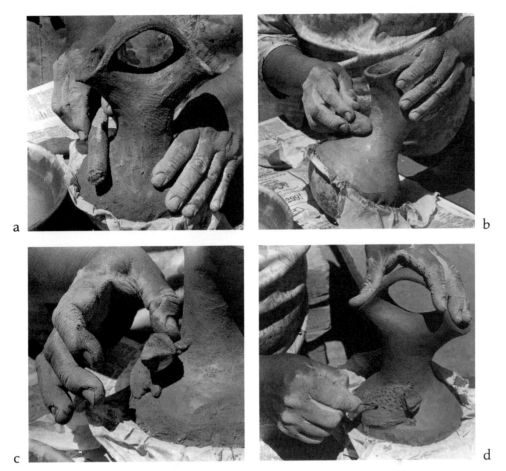

*Navajo pottery decorating and finishing techniques:* a) *scraping,* b) *polishing,*
c) *horned toad appliqué,* d) *texturing with a pin. Betty Manygoats pictured.*

complished by scraping with a corncob or shredded juniper bark, producing a somewhat roughened, scored surface.

To attain an even higher degree of surface polish, several of today's
Navajo potters delay the final polishing until the vessel has dried to the
"leather-hard" stage. At that stage, the clay is still pliable and polishing
serves to align the clay particles parallel to the surface and to drive bits of
tempering material deep beneath the surface, resulting in a much smoother
finish. This technique has long been used by Pueblo potters.

The next step in the manufacturing process involves decorating the

19

Left, *appliqué detail on a pot by John Whiterock (Navajo Tribal Museum collection), and,* right, *a decorative fillet with the traditional ceremonial break in a pot by Alice Cling (Collection of Jan Musial)*

vessel. Several techniques are available to the potter and it is rare to find a vessel that has not been decorated using a combination of at least two techniques, including appliqué, modeling, incising, or stamping. For the purpose of discussion, however, each of these techniques will be described separately.

Appliqué is among the oldest decorative techniques used by Navajo potters and requires the addition of clay to the exterior surface of an otherwise finished vessel, much as a coil would be added to build up a vessel's height. This additional clay is fashioned into any shape desired and is sometimes further embellished. The most common decorative element applied using this technique is a clay band called a fillet. Although found today on most Navajo vessels, the fillet's origin is not known. Navajo wares with clay fillets have been found in the Gobernador region at sites possibly dating as early as 1740 (Carlson 1965:65), but its use was not a common Navajo practice until ca. 1800 (Brugge 1981:14).

The clay fillet usually encircles a vessel just below the rim and its ends are not joined. It can be a single, double, or triple band; straight, wavy, or zigzagged; plain, incised, or stamped. The "ceremonial break" left in the design is analogous to the "spirit line" found on many Navajo rugs and baskets; that is, it prevents the maker's creative energies from being entrapped in that particular item, thus preventing her or him from making additional rugs, baskets, or pots.

Appliqué is undoubtedly the favored decorative technique among today's contemporary Navajo potters and it presents endless opportunities for individual creativity. Popular animal and floral motifs include horned toads, sheep and other domestic animals, cacti, pine cones, oak leaves, acorns, corn, and others, many of which are extremely realistic and highly detailed. A few potters have used the technique to create entire scenes on the side of a vessel, such as a woman herding sheep, horses inside a corral, or a Navajo domestic scene with hogans and sheep. Generally, the appliqué technique is best suited for low-relief decorative elements.

A second technique as old as appliqué, or perhaps even predating it, is that of modeling. Using this technique, a potter forms the decorative element by scraping together or mounding clay from the vessel's actual walls. This is another method by which a decorative fillet can be formed. Today's potters also use the modeling technique to produce high-relief decorative elements, such as three-dimensional animal heads, that are sculpted as part of the actual pot, or fashioned separately, then attached to the vessel using the previously discussed appliqué technique. Modeling is also employed to produce a variety of free-standing, three-dimensional animal figurines, such as sheep, goats, horses, bears, and horned toads.

 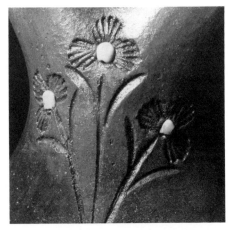

21

Left, *incising detail in a pot by Jimmy Wilson, and,* right, *stamping detail with turquoise inlay on a pot by Cecelia Whiterock (Navajo Tribal Museum collection).*

Incising is a third decorative technique and requires nothing more than a pointed stick or similar tool. The pointed end is dragged through the wet clay surface of a vessel to produce shallow lines of any desired length and shape. Although at least one potter today employs incising as a primary decorative technique, it is more commonly used as a secondary technique to further embellish and/or outline appliquéd elements. Fillets, for example, are often decorated with a series of short, incised strokes. This is also the means by which most Navajo potters inscribe their names or initials on the bases of their pots.

Closely related to incising is a fourth technique, that of stamping. This can be done with one's fingernail or the blunt end of a stick, either of which can be pressed into the soft clay and withdrawn, leaving an impression. By repeating the process, a potter can produce more complex designs, such as flowers or a repetitive band of the same design element. A few of today's potters use silversmithing die tools to produce even more delicate stamped patterns.

A fifth and final technique requiring manipulation of the clay is that of carving. Probably best practiced by potters at Santa Clara Pueblo, this is a relatively new technique to Navajo potters and one that is used by only a few individuals. As the term implies, the technique requires the removal of a portion of the clay from a vessel, much like sculpting. Among the few Navajo potters who do employ it, carving is used to produce geometric decorative elements and recessed cliff-dwelling scenes. At least one potter

*Carving detail. Pot by Elsie Black (Navajo Tribal Museum collection)*

has attempted to imitate the Santa Clara Pueblo carved style but with only limited success.

There are also several other decorative techniques in current, though limited, use by Navajo potters. One is the use of turquoise and coral inlay. To date, small nuggets or beads of these materials have appeared as the centers of floral motifs or medallion-like designs or as eyes on animal figurines. The nuggets are pressed into the wet surface of a vessel or figurine and then removed until the piece is fired, after which they are reinserted and glued in place.

Since the mid-1700s, Navajo tradition has increasingly dictated against the production of painted wares, except for use in certain ceremonies. The last traditional Navajo potter to make such painted wares died sometime around 1955 (William Beaver, personal communication to author, 20 June 1986). The idea of painted wares, however, has been revived by at least two contemporary Navajo potters who are producing nontraditional, un-pitched wares that are painted with natural pigments and paints made from boiled wild spinach *(Cleome serrulata)*, also known as beeplant.

When a piece of pottery is finished, including the decorating and polishing, it must be set aside and allowed to dry thoroughly before it can be fired. If it is not, any moisture in the clay could cause it to break or even explode during the firing process. The length of time required for a pot to dry varies from a few hours to a few days, depending upon the size and thickness of the pot, and upon weather conditions, such as the humidity level. Pots may be dried outdoors or inside the hogan, next to or even atop a stove. Minor cracks that appear during the drying process are repaired by applying a small amount of wet clay.

Once the pots are thoroughly dried, they are ready for the most crucial stage of the entire manufacturing process, that of firing. All potters have their own preferred methods, depending upon their own experiences and by whom they were first taught. The most traditional method is to build a small fire of juniper on the open ground and allow it to burn down. The hot coals are then raked over and the pottery is placed on top and completely covered with additional juniper and/or sheep or cattle manure. Enough fuel is added to produce a fire that will burn very hot for up to several hours, although some potters fire their pots for a much shorter length of time.

A number of potters interviewed by the author now fire their pots in a

23

*Firing and pitching Navajo pots:* a) *firing in a 55-gallon-drum kiln with juniper fuel, pitch melting in the coffee can;* b) *removing the pot from the kiln;* c) *pitching the Navajo wedding vase;* d) *removing the excess pitch. Betty Manygoats pictured.*

24

*Detail of Navajo pot showing firecloud. Pot by Louise Goodman (Collection of Jan Musial)*

cast-iron stove, using a combination of juniper and coal as fuel. In the Shonto–Cow Springs area, this can probably be explained, in part, by the close proximity to the Peabody Coal Mine on Black Mesa and the free availability of coal to Navajos. Because coal burns much hotter than juniper, its use also shortens the necessary firing time and is thus a labor-saving practice. One potter reported that coal-fired pots need only be fired once, whereas wood-fired pots ought to be fired several times to insure their durability.

After the fire has burned completely down, the pots are removed with a long stick and allowed to cool slightly. The next step is to apply a thin coating of melted piñon pitch, both inside and out. For this, a rag is wrapped around the end of a stick and the melted pitch is liberally brushed over the interior and exterior surfaces. Excess pitch is wiped off and the pot is then allowed to cool completely.

25

Although the real purpose for the pitch coating is to make the vessel waterproof, it serves a cosmetic purpose as well. When first removed from the fire, Navajo pottery is a dull color ranging from tan to gray to black.

Also common on Navajo pottery are random gray and black markings called fireclouds, caused by the pot's coming into direct contact with the burning fuel. The pitch coating applied after the pot is fired not only gives Navajo pottery its characteristic dark brown color and lustre, but also brings out the random patterns of these fireclouds, adding to the subtle beauty. The pitch gives off a sweet fragrance that sometimes lasts for several months.

With the addition of the pitch coating, most Navajo pots are ready for use or sale. For a few potters, however, one final step remains. The decorative techniques discussed so far have all been prefiring techniques. Within the past decade, however, several new postfiring techniques have also been developed. At least two potters now paint portions of their pots after they have been fired, using enamel or acrylic paints. Such painting is generally confined to small appliquéd elements such as flowers, sheep, clouds, or similar motifs. When used sparingly, the result can be pleasing, but when used excessively, the paints overpower or even mask the sculptural qualities of the underlying appliqué work.

Sandpainting, too, has entered the pottery tradition in the work of several potters. During the 1930s, a technique was developed to preserve in permanent form the beautiful drypaintings that are created and then subsequently destroyed during Navajo healing ceremonies. The technique bonds sand and other dry pigments to a support (usually particle board) by means of an undercoating of glue or other adhesive. The first use of this technique on handmade pottery occurred during the late 1970s, at which time simple, geometric designs were applied after the pots were pitched. These have gradually given way to more and more elaborate designs that cover the entire surface of a vessel, thus eliminating entirely the need to pitch the vessel.

# CHAPTER 4

# HISTORIC NAVAJO POTTERY

SINCE THE LATE 1800S, pottery has been among the principal artifact types used by southwestern archaeologists to unravel the region's complex cultural history, which requires an understanding not only of the many individual cultural groups but also of their interactions with each other. In comparison with the often finely crafted and sometimes beautifully painted prehistoric Pueblo wares, whose origins can be traced back in time more than one thousand years, most historic Navajo pottery is plain and often crudely made. This, coupled with the fact that the Navajo entered the Southwest relatively recently, may partially account for the limited attention that archaeologists have given to early Navajo studies, especially in the all-important Dinétah region of northwestern New Mexico. Much of the work done to date relating to early Navajo pottery has been the result of land claims cases or of survey and/or mitigation activities conducted within project-specific boundaries (Brugge 1981; Farmer 1942; Dittert 1958; Cella et al. 1984). Little systematic work has been done in the Dinétah area, despite the rapid destruction of sites as a result of intense energy-development-related activities.

Although Navajo pottery has been largely resistant to change during the past few centuries, it has not been entirely so. Several major changes have been identified within the Navajo pottery tradition, allowing archaeologists to construct a general Navajo pottery sequence. Even today, however, this sequence is far from complete. A great deal of work still remains to be done in order to refine it and to account for the full range of

27

variation found in Navajo pottery across the extensive area known as Navajoland.

Ceramic typologies are tools used by archaeologists to denote similarities and possible relationships between different pottery styles. They are based on physical traits, such as temper or designs, that are common to a number of pottery vessels within a geographical region. The extent of these areas will vary in relation to aboriginal population densities, the degree of intragroup movement, and the level of trade or other social interaction among neighboring groups. Traits such as the use of sherd temper instead of sand temper, or the use of certain designs, often relate closely to group identity, as evidenced by historic Pueblo pottery. By statistically comparing the occurrence of defined pottery types at a particular site or over a larger area, archaeologists can determine a relative date or range of dates when the site or area was occupied, as well as the degree to which the original inhabitants interacted with other groups. Other dating techniques, such as tree-ring analysis or radiocarbon analysis, can provide even more precise dates.

In the case of the Navajo, it is known that they lived in more or less independent extended family groups with no real sense of tribal identity until the late eighteenth century. Navajo contact with other groups, especially Pueblo groups, can be documented by the occurrence of Pueblo wares at early Navajo sites.

The handing down of the pottery tradition within each family group thus insured a certain degree of homogeneity of the pottery. Overall, the limited range of Navajo vessel forms and designs was guided by tradition. The changes that will be described in this chapter are, for the most part, attributable to influences from outside the Navajo culture, and they allow archaeologists to identify several major pottery types within the historic Navajo pottery tradition. The list, however, is by no means complete. For every type described, there are several subtypes that differ perhaps in only one trait and thus do not merit separate type names. Readers interested in more detailed and technical descriptions of the various historic Navajo pottery types are referred to Brugge (1981:3–12).

## DINÉTAH GRAY

The earliest type of Navajo pottery identified by archaeologists is designated as Dinétah Gray. Found throughout the Dinétah area, vessel

*Dinétah Gray jar, ca. early to mid-1700s (Navajo Tribal Museum collection)*

forms of this type include bowls and large jars with somewhat pointed bottoms, greatly expanded midsections, and wide constricted necks with flaring rims. Vessel walls are usually relatively thin and sometimes crumbly as a result of the abundant sand temper. Interior and exterior surfaces were typically wiped with shredded juniper bark or corncobs, producing a rough texture. Colors range from gray to black. The range of Dinétah Gray wares in northwestern New Mexico and northeastern Arizona extends from the Puerco River of the East (a tributary to the Rio Grande River) to Canyon de Chelly.

Dinétah Gray vessels were occasionally decorated with incised lines or fillets, but most vessels lack any decoration at all. The type was produced primarily between 1700 and 1800, but many archaeologists suspect that its presence has gone unnoticed on some sites where it has been misidentified as an Anasazi utility ware, further confounding attempts to understand early Navajo history. Its decline in production during the latter part of the eighteenth century and its gradual replacement by Navajo Gray and Pinyon Gray wares (described below) correspond to the growing importance of herding as a part of the Navajo economy. Herding necessitated an increasing degree of mobility on the part of the Navajo, but Dinétah Gray wares were unsuitable for transport because of their weak construction and large size.

## GOBERNADOR POLYCHROME

Toward the end of the 1600s, many Pueblo people, especially from Jemez Pueblo, took refuge with the Navajo for fear of Spanish reprisals for the successful 1680 Pueblo Revolt (Forbes 1960:270–72). Gobernador Polychrome pottery is a direct result of this union that saw Navajo and Pueblo people living within single compounds. Vessel forms of this type are decidedly Pueblo in origin and include squat jars with wide but short, tapering necks and steep-sided bowls. Some of the red, orange, and black geometric motifs that are found on Gobernador Polychrome vessels appear to be clearly derived from earlier Jemez pottery (Carlson 1965: 56,100).

The period of greatest production of Gobernador Polychrome vessels was the first half of the eighteenth century, the type having developed first in the Navajo Reservoir District and only later in Gobernador and Largo canyons to the south (Dittert 1958:18; Dittert, Hester, and Eddy

*Gobernador polychrome jar (University of Colorado Museum collection)*

*Navajo polychrome jar, ca. early 1800s (Navajo Tribal Museum collection)*

1961:236). These dates and geographical distributions correspond to Ute and Comanche pressures from the north and fear of Spanish attacks from the east.

## Navajo Painted/Navajo Polychrome

Directly descended from the earlier Gobernador Polychrome style, Navajo Painted wares made their appearance around 1750. Although early examples closely resemble Gobernador Polychrome, differences in the paste account for the separate designation. As the Navajo began to abandon the Dinétah region, they rejected many of the puebloan traits that had earlier been adopted. Increasingly, painted designs on pottery were done only in a single color, either red or black, on an orange or buff-colored background.

The designs on Navajo Painted wares are usually poorly executed and consist largely of simple geometric shapes. Many of the examples of this style now found in museum collections date to the twentieth century and reflect the efforts of several anthropologists to especially document this aspect of Navajo pottery making.

Traditional Navajo Painted wares should not be confused with contemporary Navajo wares that are pitched and partially painted with acrylic or enamel paints. In contrast to these, Navajo Painted wares are painted with natural pigments that, when fired, yield colors with a dull matte finish. Navajo Painted wares continued in production until the mid-1950s.

## Navajo Gray

After their emigration from the Dinétah region, the Navajo became increasingly mobile as herding gradually gained importance in their overall economy. This necessitated several important changes in Navajo pottery to make it more portable. Vessels gradually became smaller and their walls became thicker and the bases more rounded.

Navajo Gray pottery has been made since ca. 1800 in an area of northwestern New Mexico east and north of the Chuska, Carrizo, and Zuni mountain ranges. Tempered with finely ground sherds with some sand, jars and bowls range in color from light gray to black. Vessel surfaces are usually wiped and/or scraped with juniper bark, cornhusks, or a corncob

*Navajo Gray jar, ca. mid- to late 1800s (Navajo Tribal Museum collection)*

and are decorated with single, double, or triple appliquéd (occasionally modeled) fillets.

## Pinyon Gray

Pinyon Gray pottery is contemporaneous with Navajo Gray and is distinguishable from the latter only on the basis of abundant, coarsely ground sherd temper and the fact that decorative fillets are usually modeled rather than appliquéd. Pinyon Gray wares are found west of the Chuska, Carrizo, and Zuni mountains and extend to the western boundaries of the Navajo homeland. Even today the Chuska Mountains are a formidable divider between the eastern portion of the Navajo Reservation and the central and western portions.

# CHAPTER 5

# DECLINE AND SURVIVAL
# OF THE POTTERY TRADITION

A S WE HAVE SEEN, pottery making is an ancient tradition among the Navajo, spanning several centuries of recorded time. The traditions associated with pottery making have been passed from one generation to another, relatively unchanged, over the course of those centuries. Contacts with non-Navajo groups, a gradual shift from an agricultural economy to a herding economy, and the regional variation in the use of different clays and tempering materials throughout Navajoland accounted for gradual changes in vessel shapes and other matters of design. But overall, Navajo pottery remained more or less homogeneous well into the twentieth century.

What then caused this age-old tradition to go into a tailspin beginning in the late 1800s, that for all practical purposes nearly threatened its extinction? The answer is complex because many factors played a contributing role, and as we shall see, at least one factor that contributed to the decline of Navajo pottery was equally responsible for insuring that it was not lost entirely.

Like much of traditional Navajo material culture, pottery has very strong utilitarian roots. Quite simply, pottery was made to be used, either in a domestic or in a ceremonial context. The strongest blow to the tradition, then, came with the establishment of trading posts to serve the Navajo people, the first ones being operational even before the Navajo Reservation had been officially established in 1868. After the railroad was built along the reservation's southern boundaries in 1881, the number of such

36

posts literally skyrocketed. As each new post opened, the Navajos had greater access to more and more Anglo trade goods, including glass, metal, and crockery containers of all shapes and sizes.

The Navajos may have been slow to adopt the Anglo cash economy, but the barter system, upon which the early trading posts were built, was quite successful in helping them to acquire all sorts of Anglo products. The gradual buildup in Navajo households of Anglo-made cooking and storage containers not only lessened the need for handmade pottery, but also undermined the native pottery tradition in another way. Whereas in pre–Fort Sumner times, potters routinely passed on their pottery-making knowledge and skills to the next generation of young women, the widespread availability of Anglo trade goods planted the seeds of disinterest in even learning the craft among the younger women.

With the tremendous decline in the domestic demand for pottery, Navajo ceremonialism was left as the major support for the tradition. Navajo ceremonialism, however, is very conservative, and in relation to pottery making, this conservatism had both positive and negative effects. On the negative side, pottery and, more specifically, the making of pottery, came to be associated with numerous restrictive behaviors. Tschopik (1938:260) argues that in earlier times many of these behaviors were probably reserved only for pots intended for, or already in, use in a ceremonial context. With the loss of the domestic context, however, these behaviors were applied across the board to all pottery, and pottery itself took on strong associative powers capable of causing harm to anyone who came into contact with it, especially the person making pottery.

The list of restrictive behaviors relating to pottery making and reported in the literature is lengthy, put a partial list includes the following: 1) a woman should not allow others to observe her while making pottery but should work instead in a location away from the residential hogan; 2) she should not step over the clay or pottery-making tools while making pottery or allow others to do so; 3) she should be careful not to break the metate or animal bones while engaged in pottery making; 4) she should not molest snakes, frogs, or puppies; 5) she should not curse others or have bad thoughts about them; 6) she should not jump across deep ditches; 7) no one with bloody hands should touch the pottery; 8) menstruating women should not make pottery; 9) the pottery should not

*Navajo painted jar, ca. mid- to late 1800s (Navajo Tribal Museum collection)*

be exposed to drafts; 10) women who had had certain sings or ceremonies performed for them could not make pottery (Tschopik 1938:259, 1941:48–50; Sapir and Sandoval 1930:576).

Failure to observe these and a host of other similar restrictions was frequently cited by Navajos as cause for newly made pottery breaking or cracking. It was also given as an explanation for illnesses or other mishaps befalling women who made pottery. In his study of potters in the Ramah, New Mexico, area, Tschopik (1941:50) observed that the range of the taboos "varied from one potter to the next."

The point to be made is that as the behavior associated with pottery making became more and more restricted, fewer and fewer women were willing to learn and practice the craft, partly because they were unwilling to observe the many restrictions and partly because they feared harm to themselves even if they unknowingly failed to observe one or more of these restrictions. Among Tschopik's study group, some women were specifically told by medicine men that their health problems stemmed from their involvement in pottery making (Tschopik 1938:261). In such an atmosphere, potters became afraid to make any pots that did not fit into the very narrow design framework that the medicine men defined.

Unable or unwilling to express any individual creativity, Navajo potters, themselves, all but doomed their craft to a stable but stagnant existence. The lack of variety of vessel forms and the crudeness of Navajo pottery, in comparison with Pueblo wares, made the establishment of a commercial market virtually impossible. The attitudes of reservation traders regarding Navajo pottery also ruled out the possibility of such a market.

Markets for Navajo textiles were developed in the latter decades of the 1880s, and the demand by non-Indians for quality Indian jewelry was well established in the 1920s. Similarly, finely crafted and painted pottery from the various Pueblos had commanded the public's attention since the turn of the century. The establishment of these markets all involved non-Indian traders who were interested in the products themselves, in the economic benefits that could be derived from their sale, or both. In the case of Navajo pottery, however, no one on the reservation was interested in the craft other than a few anthropologists. Traders contemptuously referred to Navajo wares as "mud pots," for which they could envision no economic benefits, either for themselves or for the potters.

One other factor that may have contributed to a decline in pottery production, at least in some parts of the reservation, was a depletion of suitable and accessible clay deposits. This certainly seems to have been a factor in the Ramah, New Mexico, area, where several informants reported having to buy suitable clay from the Zunis (Tschopik 1941:17). Several modern-day potters living outside the Shonto–Cow Springs area now travel considerable distances to procure their clay, but before the days of paved highways on the reservation, long-distance travel to procure clay would have been unlikely. Thus the situation reported at Ramah may have occurred in other parts of the reservation as well.

Despite the seemingly overwhelming number of factors working against its survival, the Navajo pottery tradition nevertheless did survive, almost tenaciously, although it did not prosper. Let us turn now to look at those factors that helped in this regard.

First, we must again consider the role of ceremonialism. Although ceremonial restrictions were causing fewer and fewer women to make pottery, the need for pottery in certain Navajo ceremonies assured continued production to some degree. Enemy Way, for instance, requires the use of a Navajo pottery drum, and other ceremonies dictate that food for the patient must be prepared in a Navajo earthen vessel. In creating the drypaintings that are such an integral part of many Navajo healing rites, the medicine man often uses small pottery bowls and other types of containers to keep the dry pigments and medicinal herbs.

Tschopik (1941:55–65) explains at great length various instances in which pipes are ritually used by the Navajo and the circumstances surrounding their manufacture. The efficacy of many ceremonials demands the availability of Navajo pottery vessels, and unlike prayersticks and other ritual paraphernalia that can be renewed by replacing worn or damaged organic parts such as feathers, a pot or a ritual smoking pipe that has been chipped or cracked through use must often be ritually disposed of and a new one made to replace it.

It was this ceremonial need for pottery that largely sustained the craft during the first half of this century. Small bowls, jars, and pipes were the primary vessel forms in production and use during that time. But at the same time, the range in size, shape, and decoration was extremely limited, underscoring the degree to which potters conformed to group beliefs and/or fears concerning pottery manufacture.

A second factor that also played a role, albeit a limited one, in sustaining the craft during the early to middle twentieth century was a continued interest expressed by several anthropologists. During the 1930s and 1940s, material culture studies received far greater attention from anthropologists than they have in the intervening years. A review of the limited literature relating specifically to Navajo pottery quickly shows that a great deal of it dates from this period (see references, beginning on page 103).

As part of their studies, Tschopik (1941) and Hurt (1942) assembled field collections of pottery and documented other collections, many of which are illustrated in their publications. The degree to which individual pieces were documented varied, but nevertheless, these early studies are very important because they predate even the beginnings of the changes that are taking place today, and because no similar studies have been done in the intervening years.

CHAPTER 6

# THE REVITALIZATION
# OF NAVAJO POTTERY

THE ETHNOGRAPHIC LITERATURE dealing with Navajo pottery, contains frequent comments and predictions concerning the plight and dying nature of Navajo pottery (Stephen 1893:358; Tschopik 1938:258, 1941:48). Similar predictions have also been made over the years about Navajo weaving (Amsden 1934:237; Maxwell 1963:63). Some anthropologists and others writing in the past about the Navajo have underestimated both the intrinsic value of certain elements or traditions of Navajo culture to the overall cultural framework and the ability of individual Navajo craftspeople to respond to new markets.

In the case of Navajo pottery, we have seen how ritual needs were strong enough to sustain the craft long after a domestic need had ceased. But we have seen, too, that it was sustained in a very stagnant state, undergoing virtually no change over a period of at least sixty years. How then, and why, has Navajo pottery changed so much in recent years from what it was even as late as the 1960s? What events, individuals, or other factors have played a role in what can accurately be termed a revitalization of Navajo pottery?

Obviously the changes we see today in Navajo pottery did not occur over a period of just a few years. Actually, the seeds of change were planted almost two generations ago, but they took nearly twenty years to germinate. In the early 1940s, an individual named William Beaver began working at Chaco Canyon, and for whatever reasons, Navajo pottery sparked his interest. When he tried to purchase some only six years later, he discovered the trading post near Pueblo del Arroyo in Chaco Canyon

42

was gone and that two Navajo women potters in the area had both died (Beaver: personal communication to author, 20 June 1986).

Around 1949, Beaver assisted at an early Navajo Craftsman Exhibition sponsored by the Museum of Northern Arizona and noted the virtual absence of Navajo pottery. Shortly afterwards, he began working for Reuben and Mildred Heflin at the Shonto Trading Post in Shonto, Arizona. To some extent, Mrs. Heflin shared Beaver's interest in Navajo pottery, and together they let it be known that they wanted to buy some painted pottery. Much to their surprise and horror, what they received were a few pieces painted with enamel house paints! None of the local potters apparently had any knowledge of the earlier tradition of painted wares.

On another occasion while at the Shonto post, Beaver purchased three crates of pitched Navajo wares. These were eventually sold to Tucson dealer Tom Bahti; this convinced Beaver that a market for Navajo pottery could be stimulated, but not as long as reservation traders held the pots in contempt, still referring to them as "mud pots."

While employed at Shonto, Beaver began collecting examples of Navajo pottery, although he did so without any real plan to build a comprehensive collection. From the beginning, his primary interest had been in painted Navajo wares, and some of his earliest purchases of painted pottery from C. G. Wallace of Gallup and from a woman potter near Cove, Arizona, are now in the collections of the Southwest Museum in Los Angeles and the Arizona State Museum in Tucson. Years later, when Malcolm Farmer, a prominent archaeologist, told Beaver about a woman in Canyon de Chelly who made painted pottery, he tried to find her. As it turned out, the woman had died sometime around 1955, but her son showed Beaver where the woman had made her pottery, and he collected a few broken sherds as examples of the painted wares that previously had been made by the Navajo.

Over the years, Beaver continued to add to his personal collection and to purchase additional pieces for resale, especially after he opened his own business near Flagstaff. Much of the Navajo pottery that he purchased, however, was simply stockpiled because there still was little interest among dealers. Navajo people purchased some pottery from him, but overall, sales were not impressive. At this time (the early 1960s), Navajo potters were still apparently bound by the age-old beliefs and group

43

*Pottery by Chris McHorse*

pressures that prevented them from making anything but the standard jars and bowls, each one virtually the same as the next and few possessing commercial appeal.

Despite poor retail sales, wholesale business was a bit more encouraging for Beaver. Sometime in the early 1960s, an itinerant salesman of Indian material by the name of Grover Turner began buying small quantities of Navajo pottery, which he then resold throughout the western states.

What initially sparked Turner's interest in Navajo pottery, and exactly where and to whom he sold his merchandise, may never be known because Turner is no longer living. Whenever Turner's inventory was largely depleted, he would return to Flagstaff and choose additional examples before returning to the road. On these occasions, he and Beaver would discuss which items sold best and how others might be made more salable. This information was, in turn, relayed to individual potters, and gradually the pottery showed more and more variation.

Variation or change of the pottery itself was a very important step towards establishing a commercial market. Prior to the 1960s, the lack of individual creativity by Navajo potters and the overall crudeness of their work were perhaps the biggest obstacles to such a market. Getting potters to experiment and to expand their range of vessel shapes and designs, however, necessarily required a change in certain Navajo attitudes and the promise of certain financial rewards.

In the 1960s, after producing the same crude jars and bowls for decades, Navajo potters were apparently open to the necessary changes. Why? Had they suddenly decided to reject the warnings of their own people and of Navajo medicine men concerning the possible consequences of reckless behavior while engaged in pottery making?

This apparent reversal of Navajo thought was not as sudden as it might appear. Throughout this century, as the Navajo people have become increasingly acculturated, many of the ritual restrictions that previously governed their behavior have become more and more relaxed. For example, when the first yei-style rugs were woven in the early decades of this century, Navajo reactions ranged from "extreme criticism to outright apprehension regarding potential offense to the Holy People" (McGreevey 1982:12). Nevertheless, more and more weavers were willing to weave the design. Similarly, when Hosteen Klah, a well-known Navajo medicine man, wove accurate sandpainting rugs during the 1920s and 1930s, he frequently had to reassure his own people that no harm would come to him. Each of his nieces who assisted him, however, had a ceremony performed so that they, too, would escape the possible displeasure of the Holy People.

45

In the 1940s, a method was developed to preserve in permanent form the beautiful sandpaintings that were such an integral part of Navajo healing rites but which were destroyed as part of the ceremony. Parezo

(1983:75-99) has studied the mechanism by which Navajo thought gradually changed in order to make such actions acceptable and harmless for those involved. Today, hundreds of Navajos make their livings by producing, for sale, sandpaintings that depict a wide range of sacred motifs. Because these paintings are not exact copies of the ceremonial sandpaintings, however, they are considered neither sacred nor harmful.

The Navajo belief that deities should not be depicted or called upon except for legitimate ceremonial purposes is extremely strong, but the above examples demonstrate how this belief has also been circumvented on occasion. Why then were Navajo potters so slow to respond to the same factors that would have allowed them a greater degree of freedom to practice their craft? Several factors must be considered.

First, the number of Navajo potters has always been small in comparison to the number of weavers and silversmiths, and before the 1940s there were no secular sandpainters at all. Secondly, the Shonto–Cow Springs area, long the center of Navajo pottery production, was, and still is, one of the most traditional areas on the entire Navajo Reservation. Individuals there would be less likely to change long-established patterns unless a need for such a change was required within the community itself or would be of direct benefit to them. And until roads in the area were paved, area residents had only limited contact with the outside.

Throughout this century across the Navajo Reservation, increased acculturation and the ever-growing influence of traders and craft dealers have broken down certain prohibitions relating not only to pottery, but also to other crafts. Yei figures and other previously sacred motifs now appear not only on pottery, but more recently, on baskets and jewelry as well. In the Shonto–Cow Springs area, in particular, paved roads, the building of area schools, and the opening of the Peabody Coal Mine on Black Mesa and the Navajo Power Plant in Page offered the local people increased job opportunities and increased contact with people from outside the area.

The above changes relating to craft production could never have occurred in the absence of a commercial market, but the question of which came first, the commercial market or the willingness and/or ability of potters to express individual creativity, is actually a moot one. Clearly, the two had to develop simultaneously in order to nurture and sustain one another. Once a market was established, however, potters responded by decorating their pots in ways that previously would have been out of the question.

The first changes adopted by Navajo potters, in an attempt to improve the quality and variety of their products, were very simple, such as varying the incised strokes on a decorative fillet or making minor changes in the shapes of rims. As one innovation met with acceptance, it was further elaborated. As new vessel forms and designs were developed by individual potters, they were learned or imitated by others.

By the late 1960s, individual creativity began to play an important role in Navajo pottery, so that even if two potters used the same decorative elements, each added his or her own special touch. Individual potters also soon realized that they found greater enjoyment in making certain forms or that they were better skilled in executing certain designs. During the late 1960s and early 1970s, especially, the range of appliqué designs literally exploded; it was for the market to determine which ones would survive.

To further strengthen the still fledgling market, Beaver continued to enter works in the Navajo Craftsman Exhibition at the Museum of Northern Arizona. Since its inception in 1936, this annual show has been the leading showcase for Navajo crafts and has played an especially important role in the past decade in showcasing the works of contemporary Navajo potters and fostering a public appreciation for new innovations. Having potters demonstrate pottery making during the show has further educated the public, allowing them to witness firsthand the many time-consuming steps and hard work involved.

As a result of the interest generated by the Museum of Northern Arizona's annual show and of the personal interests of respective staff members, several museums have adopted collecting strategies and/or hosted exhibitions that have further bolstered the market and increased public awareness of the changes taking place. Museums in this country have been influencing the public's collecting interests in ethnographic material from the Southwest and from other areas since the late 1800s (Parezo 1986; Bell 1982), but in the case of contemporary Navajo pottery, the three museums to play a role are all in Arizona.

Not unexpectedly, the Museum of Northern Arizona was the first to focus its attention on this changing art. In 1978, then Registrar of Anthropological Collections H. Diane Wright instituted a purchasing plan to augment the museum's holdings in Navajo pottery, coupled with her own

48

*Pottery by Betty Manygoats drying in front of her hogan*
*Cow Springs, Arizona, 1987*

research relating to the craft. In 1979, the museum presented a comprehensive exhibit on Navajo pottery, tracing the history and technology of the craft and highlighting contemporary examples that had been recently acquired. The exhibit represented the first time a museum had given such attention to Navajo pottery and it opened many eyes to the true scope of the craft. The Museum of Northern Arizona is still actively adding to its permanent collection of Navajo pottery.

The Arizona State Museum at the University of Arizona in Tucson was next to show an interest in Navajo pottery. In 1981, the museum purchased Bill Beaver's Navajo pottery collection that spans the period from ca. 1950 to 1980. This collection of more than two hundred pieces is undoubtedly the most comprehensive and best documented collection of its kind, and Curator of Collections Jan Bell and H. Diane Wright are adding to the already extensive documentation that accompanies it by compiling genealogies for Navajo potters and assembling photo documentation of current pottery technology and trends.

The third and final museum to play a role in the current field of Navajo pottery is the Navajo Tribal Museum at Window Rock, Arizona. By 1981, the museum had acquired well over one hundred examples of Navajo pottery, ranging from the early eighteenth century to the early 1960s. Some of these had been collected during the Navajo Land Claims studies of the late 1950s, but overall the collection was lacking in documentation. Also, the fact that the most recent pieces dated to ca. 1964 meant that the current revitalization movement was completely unrepresented.

In 1981, the Navajo Tribal Museum began to acquire work by current Navajo potters. Since then, the museum's Navajo pottery collection has grown to approximately two hundred fifty examples. A temporary exhibit of selected contemporary pieces from the collection was installed in 1983, and again the public was surprised at the variety to be found in Navajo pottery. In 1985, with the cooperation of Jan Musial, a Flagstaff dealer in Navajo crafts, the museum hosted a month-long exhibit and sale of Alice Cling's work. Most recently a permanent exhibit of contemporary Navajo pottery was installed, including works by most of the potters discussed in chapters 7 and 8. Future plans call for continued acquisitions of works by potters not currently represented in the collection, as well as of additional innovative pieces by those who are already represented.

Around 1964–65, at the same time a market was being established for pottery produced in the Shonto–Cow Springs Area, the Rough Rock Demonstration School, located at Rough Rock, Arizona, on the eastern flanks of Black Mesa, began to offer various Navajo craft workshops, including one for pottery. Classes conducted by Helen Woody and Alta Chee, both from the Rough Rock community, were conducted daily for several weeks. When the course was completed, a different type of craft was taught for the next few weeks.

When they were first offered, these craft courses were open only to Rough Rock area residents, but when a number of other communities asked to send interested individuals, they were opened to all Navajo people. Enrollment fees for people from outside the Rough Rock community were paid by the former Office of Navajo Economic Opportunity, a federally funded tribal office that sponsored many training programs for Navajo Reservation residents during the 1960s and 1970s. Fees for Rough Rock residents, on the other hand, were paid by the school.

Over the course of two years, more than fifty Navajo women completed the pottery training classes (Roessel 1982:163). Exactly how many continued making pottery afterwards is unknown, but a number of potters are still reportedly active in and around the Rough Rock community. Few, if any, however, seem to be producing pottery for the tourist market. Instead, their work includes the standard jars, bowls, drums, and pipes that are still used by Navajo people for ceremonial purposes. This emphasis on serving the needs of the Navajo people is clearly in keeping with the school's mandate and further reflects the dichotomy of the current Navajo pottery market.

Creating a market for Navajo pottery, at least among non-Navajos, also required a change in the public's perception of the product (Wright 1980). In the previous chapter, the limited appeal of Navajo pottery was discussed as one factor that prevented the establishment of a commercial market. Why then have public attitudes changed?

First, a number of Navajo potters have improved the overall quality of their work by making vessels more symmetrical in terms of overall shape and thickness. They are also paying greater attention to individual details of the vessel's form, such as the handle or the rim, and are varying these to add more interest.

Variation and innovations in vessel forms and decorative elements help to identify the work of individual potters, but in any art form, some collectors are interested in the work of only one or two potters, while others may be interested more in shapes or designs and less with the maker's identity. A Navajo pot today can appeal to a collector on a variety of levels, even to someone who does not necessarily collect Indian art.

The brown coloration of Navajo pitch-coated pottery and the random firecloud patterns reflect the natural beauty of the clay and perhaps speak most eloquently about the strong ties that exist between the Navajo potter and Mother Earth. To be sure, Pueblo potters feel these same ties, but the vibrant and colorful Pueblo designs sometimes overpower the natural beauty of the clay itself. The overall plain color of Navajo pitch-coated pottery, even if decorated with appliquéd or incised motifs, blends more easily with a variety of decors than does Pueblo pottery.

Once the market had been established for Navajo pottery, certain factors were also necessary to maintain a certain level of production. Price was, and is, one of those factors. Since the 1950s, when it was possible to buy an entire crate of Navajo pottery for only a few dollars, prices have steadily increased, but even today, most Navajo pottery is priced considerably lower than Pueblo pots of comparable size. Higher quality and more creative works produced by the better-known Navajo potters are, of course, commanding higher prices, even exceeding the magical four-figure mark in some cases.

A ready supply of clay and potters to work the clay are even more vital to sustaining the craft. The clay deposit used by most potters in the Shonto–Cow Springs area has been mined for many years and shows no sign of depletion. Other sources in the area and in several other locations on and around Black Mesa are also used.

As for potters, the number is steadily increasing as the market for pottery expands. The list of currently active Navajo potters includes individuals from every age group, and in the Shonto–Cow Springs area, most of the potters are related to each other either directly or through marriage or clan affiliation. These relationships still seem to be the principal avenues by which pottery-making skills are passed from generation to generation.

Individual creativity is also playing an important role in strengthening the market. Potters such as Alice Cling, Faye Tso, and Jimmy Wilson have developed unique styles in their work and are thus commanding the highest prices, while work by other potters remains more moderately priced.

Exactly what makes one person's work more collectible than that of another is sometimes difficult to identify, but overall quality and uniqueness are certainly key factors.

Many, though not all, of the potters involved in the current commercial market have at some point signed some of their work. No one, however, is absolutely consistent in this regard, and a few potters who have signed their work for several years have recently stopped doing so. For those whose style is rather unique, a signature is really not necessary, but the decision not to sign one's work may also be related to the widespread Navajo fear that someone could use a signed pot to witch the maker. Fear of witchcraft may also be related to the general reluctance of potters to enter their work in competitions, but a more plausible explanation is the need to immediately convert finished craft products into cash, rather than consign them to competitions where sales cannot be guaranteed.

Before turning to a discussion of the individual potters and their works, one more point must be mentioned in relation to sustaining and even nurturing the present market. Although the Santa Fe Indian Market played no role in initially creating a demand for Navajo pottery, the participation at the market by contemporary Navajo potters Alice Cling (represented in 1983 and 1984 by her daughter, Donna), Christine McHorse (1983–present), Lucy McKelvey (1975–present), and Jimmy Wilson (1981–present) has certainly broadened the base of public awareness of, and appreciation for, contemporary Navajo pottery in its various styles.

As the leading annual competition for Indian artists, the Santa Fe Indian Market attracts thousands of visitors and collectors each year. The continued presence of Navajo potters at the market is certain to have a continuing positive effect upon the entire field of Navajo pottery as more and more people come to realize that Navajo pottery has changed dramatically in recent years and is still in an exciting developmental state. Perhaps in partial recognition of these changes, 1985 Indian Market organizers invited Dan Goodman of Mexicn Hat, Utah, to demonstrate Navajo pottery making.

# CHAPTER 7

# CONTEMPORARY PITCH–COATED NAVAJO POTTERY

**P**ERHAPS THE MOST IMPORTANT link in any craft or art form is the artist. Without individual creativity and an atmosphere in which to express that creativity, a craft becomes stagnant, at best. The Navajo pottery tradition has survived for centuries because there was a ceremonial and/or a domestic need for the product among tribal members, but during much of that time, the tradition showed no growth or vitality. The current revitalization is not the result of an increased need for pottery by the Navajos, themselves, but rather of a growing demand for Navajo pottery by non-Navajos, spurred by the development of a commercial market.

Responding to that market and to the public's demand for their wares, while at the same time recognizing the opportunity for additional income (Russell 1981; Russell and McDonald 1982), a growing number of Navajo women, and more recently men, young and old alike, have chosen the medium of clay to best express themselves artistically. Some of these individuals have actually been making pottery for many years for traditional Navajo use; others have taken up the craft more recently in response to the developing commercial market. Overall, the number of Navajo potters is still small in comparison to the number of people engaged in the more established Navajo arts of weaving and silversmithing.

Commercialization of Navajo pottery has allowed these potters to experiment in many ways. Whereas traditional Navajo use of pottery required only two basic vessel forms, namely bowls and jars, the potters who will be discussed in the following pages have introduced many varia-

53

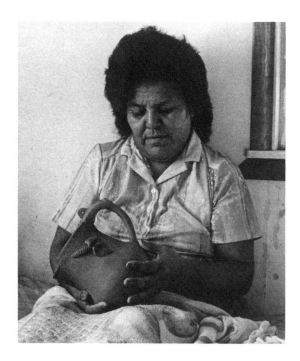

*Lorena Bartlett*
*Cow Springs, Arizona, 1986*

tions of these two forms, including some with multiple spouts and/or handles and others with unique rim and neck shapes. Effigy forms, too, are produced in a wide variety. Perhaps even more exciting is the range of decorative elements found on contemporary Navajo pottery. More often than not, the traditional clay fillet around the neck is still present, but its treatment, and even its positioning on a vessel, show a great degree of individual creativity.

The pottery that will be discussed and illustrated in this chapter differs, in many respects, from what is generally considered traditional Navajo pottery. What is important to note, however, is that these wares and their makers are closely linked to the centuries-old Navajo pottery tradition. The introduction of new vessel forms and decorative elements is merely an updating, refinement, and even an expansion of that tradition to meet the requirements of an entirely new market. The continued use of the traditional clay fillet in all its new forms, the color of the pottery, and the final application of the piñon pitch coating all serve to mark these new forms as being unmistakably Navajo.

*"Bubble pots," by Lorena Bartlett (Jan Musial collection)*

The potters whose works are discussed in this chapter have been selected on the basis of their overall contributions to the current field of pitch-coated Navajo pottery. They are by no means the only Navajo potters who are making wares for sale to non-Navajos, but they account for the largest share of the market and for the greatest number of innovations that have occurred within the past two decades. Let us turn now to a more detailed look at them and their work.

LORENA H. BARTLETT, a member of the Deeshchii'nii (Start of the Red Streak People) clan, has made pottery since the late 1940s but has been involved in the tourist market for a considerably shorter time. Like other Shonto–Cow Springs potters, she gathers her clay locally, uses sherd temper, and fires her wares in a cast-iron stove.

Lorena's range of vessels is extensive and includes jars and bowls of various sizes, effigy banks in the shape of pigs, birds, and other animals, and various sculpted figures, such as buffalo. One of her specialties is large

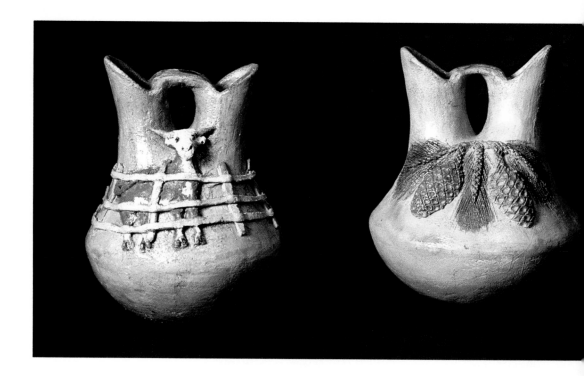

globular jars without handles, which she calls "bubble pots." She claims to have been among the first to make pitchers, some with lids, and also introduced vessels with multiple openings in the sides for use as pencil holders or flower vases. Lorena's work is often decorated with elaborate appliqué work, especially pine-cone and pine-branch motifs.

Lorena has taught her four daughters, Anita, Lula, Gloria, and Lavina, as well as her son Eugene, to make pottery, and all of her children assist her by collecting the clay, firing the pots, and applying the pitch. Occasionally, Lorena signs her work with "LHB" or "L. Bartlett" incised on the base, but more often than not she fires them unsigned. In 1984, she won a blue ribbon for her work at the Big Lake Trading Post Indian Fair near Page, Arizona.

BERTHA AND SILAS CLAW, members of the Lók'aa' dine'é (Reed People) and Tódích'íi'nii (Bitter Water) clans, respectively, are related, by clan affiliation, to several other potters in the Shonto–Cow Springs area, but they

*Pot by Alice Cling (Collection of Jan Musial)*

decorative elements has been revolutionized by Alice to conform to and complement the overall vessel shape.

Even more striking than the decoration on her pots, however, is the sheen. Before each pot is fired, it is polished to a high gloss. After Alice's pots are fired, they are given the traditional coating of piñon pitch. Any excess pitch is immediately wiped off with waxed paper, giving each vessel the color, appearance, and feel of a fine bronze casting.

Alice has demonstrated her skills to countless people at the Museum of Northern Arizona's Navajo Craftsman Exhibition in recent years, where she has also won numerous awards. In 1978, she captured the Best in Navajo Pottery award at the Heard Museum's annual Indian craft show, and in 1983 and 1984, her daughter, Donna, represented her at the Santa Fe Indian Market, where she won additional awards.

One of Alice's latest innovations is the use of red clay paint that sometimes covers the entire upper or lower half of a vessel or is wiped on in broad bands to form geometric patterns, rather than formal designs. The addition of the pitch coating over the red clay brings out its deep color, adding even more interest.

Currently, Alice signs most of her work (a few pieces are still left unsigned) by incising her first name in script form on the base, but earlier works include her initials "AC," or "Alice Cling," "Alice Williams Cling," or "Alice Williams," all incised in block letters on the base. In the late 1970s and early 1980s, at the request of a dealer, she also signed a few pieces with a black felt-tipped pen.

KATE DAVIS, a member of the Deeschii'nii (Start of the Red Streak People) clan, was only 14 years old when her grandmother, Selena Williams, taught her how to make pottery. Now in her 60s, Kate is related to several other potters in the Shonto–Cow Springs area. Lorena Bartlett and Lorena's sister, Elsie Black, are Kate's nieces, and Helen Herder is married to Kate's uncle, John Herder.

Like many other potters, Kate also uses the popular appliquéd pine-cone motif, but her best work is decorated with a simple stamped scallop design made with the end of a rounded stick. The repetition of this mark over large areas of a vessel or over the entire surface produces an interesting visual effect.

Kate is one of the few potters who still prefers to fire her pots out-

*Kate Davis*
*Cow Springs, Arizona, 1986*

*Pot by Kate Davis*
*(Navajo Tribal Museum collection)*

doors, although she sometimes uses the stove in her house to dry vessels before firing them. Because her grandmother taught her that pottery made during the winter would crack, she restricts her pottery making to the other seasons of the year. She was also taught that animals should not be depicted on pots, and so she refrains from using decorative animal motifs that are so popular with other potters.

Kate's daughter, Mary Lou Davis, has also learned the craft from her mother, and her pots and designs are very similar to her mother's.

PENNY EMERSON belongs to the Tódích'íí'nii (Bitter Water) clan and is originally from the St. Michaels, Arizona, area, although she lived in the Tuba City area for many years. She learned to make pottery approximately seven years ago from Faye Tso, and her work shows very graceful lines, whether she is doing a traditional vessel form or a more contemporary piece.

At the present time, Penny does not have her own clay source, and in the past, she has had to buy clay from other potters, sometimes premixed with the temper. Because of this and her full-time job as director of the

64

*Penny Emerson*
*Window Rock, Arizona,*
*1986*

*Pottery by Penny Emerson (Navajo Tribal Museum collection)*

Navajo Nation Family Planning Program, she does not produce a large volume of work. In a few years, however, she may devote all of her energies to her craftwork. She is also an excellent basket weaver and bead worker, and most recently has done a bit of silversmithing.

Reversing tradition a bit, Penny has taught her mother, Nesbah Emerson, to make pottery, although she says her mother was familiar with the craft to some extent before Penny became interested. Penny's concern for Navajo traditions is evident when she talks about her craftwork, speaking freely about the need to be in the proper frame of mind when one works. She says this is especially important when making pottery, because the clay senses a potter's feelings and will not turn out right if the potter is not in a state of harmony.

Penny is one of the few Navajo potters who prefers to use sand temper in her work. Her range of vessel forms is very large, including traditional jars of all sizes, pitchers, teapots, and a variety of effigy figures, including horses, horned toads, and others. Some of her best work is scraped very smooth and polished before being fired and pitched. Decoration is kept to a minimum, but might include either appliquéd, incised, or stamped designs.

To date, her work has won awards at the New Mexico State Fair and the Navajo Nation Fair. In 1981 and 1982, she also exhibited her pottery at the Eight Northern Pueblos Annual Craftsman Show, where she had previously shown her baskets. She hopes to be able to participate in more shows in coming years.

Louise R. Goodman, a member of the Bįįh bitoodnii (Deer Spring) clan, learned pottery making from Lorena Bartlett, whose brother Eddie Good-

*Pottery by Louise Goodman (Collection of Jan Musial)*

*Louise Goodman*
*Cow Springs, Arizona, 1986*

man Sr. is Louise's husband. Louise has been a potter for approximately fourteen years and is among the most prolific and versatile of today's Navajo potters. Her range of vessels includes the standard jars and bowls, but these are produced in a wide array of shapes, including a seemingly limitless range of modeled animal forms, such as chickens, rams, and a few rather exotic species. Effigy figures include dogs, squirrels, bears, lions, elephants, and a host of other domestic or wild creatures.

Perhaps the most innovative style developed by Louise is one in which the coils are obliterated only on the interior surface. This is accomplished by building up one or two coils at a time and scraping the interior of the vessel. A board shaped like an oversized ping-pong paddle is then used to tamp down the coils from the top, leaving the exterior completely unaltered. Sometimes entire jars are built up in this manner; other times only the neck or portions of a vessel are so constructed. Because each coil encircles a vessel only once (the end being pinched off and joined to the beginning), the edges or lines of the coils do not spiral around a vessel, but only encircle it.

Louise has won awards at the Museum of Northern Arizona and at the Heard Museum. Her busiest season is the summer; during the winter she

67

68

*Pottery by Louise Goodman (Collection of Jan Musial)*

only makes pottery for special orders. Some of her pots are signed with her incised initials "LRG," but like others, she says she "sometimes forgets." Following in their mother's footsteps are daughters Virginia Shortman, Stella, Alberta, and Elouise Goodman, and sons Eddie Goodman Jr. and Edward Goodman. The latter has recently begun to fashion some of his jars into electric lamps.

Betty Manygoats, a member of the Táchii'nii (Red Running into the Water People) clan, learned to make pottery approximately fourteen years ago from her paternal grandmother. She is another very prolific potter from the Shonto–Cow Springs area. Her work includes jars, bowls, and double-spouted wedding vases up to twelve inches in height. More recently, she has begun producing double-spouted jars as large as twenty inches in height and covered with as many as twenty horned-toad figures.

Betty employs perhaps the widest range of appliquéd motifs on her pottery, including horned toads, sheep, hogans, cactus, yucca, horses, and people, all of which are usually done in low relief. Some of these motifs are painted with household paints to add variety, a practice Betty adopted about ten years ago. She also makes a number of animal figures,

*Betty Manygoats*
*Cow Springs, Arizona, 1986*

69

*Pottery by Betty Manygoats*

including horses, cows, and sheep. Some of her work is signed with her initials "BM" or "BBM" (Betty Barlow Manygoats), either incised or written with a felt-tipped pen, but most of her pots are unsigned.

Betty has won awards at both the Museum of Northern Arizona and the Inter-Tribal Indian Ceremonial in Gallup. Like other potters, however, she herself has never entered her own work at these or any other competitions. She has also taught her daughters, Elizabeth, Evelyn, Elsie, Rose, and Rita, to make pottery.

FAYE AND EMMETT TSO, of Tuba City, both learned to make pottery about thirty years ago from Rose Williams, who is Emmett's aunt. Faye is of the Naakaii dine'é (Mexican, or Wondering, People) clan and Emmett is of the Lók'aa' dine'é (Reed People) clan. Of all the potters interviewed by the author, the Tsos spoke most readily about the significance of pottery within traditional Navajo culture and its place within Navajo oral history.

Unlike most Navajo potters who gather their clay near Cow Springs, the Tsos collect theirs from near Blue Canyon and from another location on Black Mesa. When working with the clay, they are ever conscious of the need to respect it. The Holy People gave the Navajo people the clay

*Emmett and Faye Tso, 1987*

*Pot by Faye Tso (Keams Canyon collection)*

*Melon pot by Faye Tso (Navajo Tribal Museum collection)*

and taught them how to form it into pottery, but they [the Holy People] are always watching to insure that the potter behaves as he or she should.

Both Faye and Emmett Tso are perhaps best known for their very large pear-shaped jars that are decorated with elaborate appliqué work, including yei and yei-bi-chai figures, corn motifs, buffalo, corn maidens, and geometric designs. A red clay slip is often applied over the entire exterior surface of large pots to further accentuate the appliquéd design. Some of their jars measure as much as three feet in height and require the use of a certain type of clay because of their weight. One such jar made by Emmett appeared on a float in former President Nixon's inaugural parade, but, unfortunately, was later destroyed in a house fire. Emmett also makes slender cylindrical jars with tall, tapered necks.

73

The Tsos fire their pottery outdoors using wood and coal as the fuel. After the pots are fired and pitched, they are soaked in water overnight to test their durability. Much of their pottery is made for Navajo ceremonial use and their close ties to Navajo traditions and practices are underscored by Faye's busy practice as an herbalist, a job that sometimes leaves her little time to make pottery. One of their sons is also a practicing Night Chant medicine man.

The Tsos began signing their work around 1973, and among all the Navajo potters, they are probably the most consistent in this respect, although even when they occasionally forget to sign a piece, their unique appliquéd motifs would identify it as their work. Their signatures are incised in script or block letters on the base of a vessel and appear as "Faye Tso, Navajo" or "Emmett Tso (or E. Tso), Navajo." Sometimes the notation "Made in USA" and the year are also included. Collaborative pieces are signed "Made by Emmett Tso (or E. Tso) family."

Almost all of the Tso children, including Darryl, Irving, Reed, Jimmy, Myra, Tina, Deanna, and Violet, have learned to make pottery from their parents. Grandson "Toto" and granddaughter Sami Lynn have also made a few pots. At the 1986 Navajo Craftsman Exhibition at the Museum of Northern Arizona, Faye and several other family members demonstrated their craft.

CECELIA AND JOHN WHITEROCK, mother and son, are related to some of the other Shonto–Cow Springs area potters through the Áshįįhi (Salt People) clan. John remembers watching his grandmother, Mary Whiterock, making pottery when he was a child, and she encouraged him to try. Now in his 20s, John began making pottery around 1979 and later taught his mother.

The clay is the first distinguishing feature of the Whiterocks' pottery. Collected on Black Mesa, it has a very smooth and creamy texture, and when fired and pitched, has the appearance of caramel candy. The next element that sets their pottery apart from that of other potters is the decoration. Cecelia usually stamps her work, using silversmithing dies to produce delicate multipetaled flowers. Turquoise nuggets and other polished stones are sometimes pressed into the centers of these flowers. Most recently, she has also produced wedding vases with incised hogan motifs and appliquéd corn motifs.

*John and Cecelia Whiterock
Cow Springs, Arizona, 1986*

*Pots by Cecelia Whiterock
(Navajo Arts and Crafts Enterprise,*
left and center; *Navajo Tribal
Museum collection,* right)

76

*Pot by John Whiterock (Navajo Tribal Museum collection)*

John's work, on the other hand, is usually decorated with floral appliqués that are more elaborate and detailed than those of other potters. Around 1981, he also began to decorate some of his pottery with simple geometric designs done in the sandpainting medium. His use of this medium will be discussed at greater length in Chapter 8.

ROSE WILLIAMS, 67 years old and of the Lók'aa' dine'é (Reed People) clan, is among the oldest potters in the Shonto–Cow Springs area, having learned to make pottery about thirty-five years ago. A very traditional Navajo woman who speaks only a few words of English, Rose lives in a small frame house. Next to it is a brush shelter where she makes most of her pottery, firing it in a cast-iron stove.

Rose has won awards at the Inter-Tribal Indian Ceremonial in Gallup, New Mexico, at the Navajo Craftsman Exhibition at the Museum of Northern Arizona in Flagstaff, and at the Heard Museum in Phoenix. In 1986, one of her large, traditionally shaped jars was awarded top honors in the pottery division at the Navajo Nation Fair in Window Rock, Arizona.

*Rose Williams, 1986*

78

*Pot by Rose Williams (Collection of Jan Musial)*

*Pot by Rose Williams (Navajo Tribal Museum collection)*

Although she, herself, has never entered work at any of these shows (dealers and collectors enter work for her) and never signs any of her work, she is obviously proud of it.

She recalls that non-Navajos began taking an interest in her work about twenty years ago, and although most of her sales continue to be to non-Navajos, many Navajos also come to her when they need pottery for ceremonial use. Rose began making large cylindrical jars, some measuring more than twenty-four inches in height and twelve inches in diameter, during the last decade. These have now become a specialty of hers. Some sport graceful handles, while others are devoid of all decoration except the traditional clay fillet encircling the vessel near the rim. She also makes pipes.

Rose has taught three of her daughters, Alice Williams Cling, Susie Williams, and Sue Williams Spencer, as well as granddaughter Donna Williams, to make pottery. Various family members help her by collecting the clay for her and polishing and pitching the pots.

JIMMY WILSON, of the Naakaii dine'é (Mexican, or Wondering, People) clan, lives near Leupp, Arizona, and is a clan relative of Faye Tso, from whom he learned to make pottery sometime around 1974 or 1975. Although Wilson makes plain traditional pottery for Navajo ceremonial use, he is best known for an elaborate, decorative style that is totally unlike that of any of the other potters.

In the late 1970s, he decorated most of his work with shallow incised designs, including geometrics and figures such as yeis. Large but well-executed appliqué motifs, such as oak leaves or yei-bi-chai dancers, also

*Jimmy Wilson at
Santa Fe Indian Market,
1986*

*Pot by Jimmy Wilson (Navajo Tribal Museum collection)*

*Pot by Jimmy Wilson*

appeared on his pots at that time. In the years since then, his incised designs have become much bolder and more elaborate, sometimes covering the entire surface of a vessel. The designs are frequently arranged within horizontal bands, the backgrounds of which are finely textured with short incised strokes. Other bands are sometimes outlined with small stamped designs, similar to those used by silversmiths.

Adding even more interest to Wilson's work is his frequent use of clay-slip paints made from different types of clay collected near his home or from locations in the Flagstaff area and from Black Mesa. These are carefully applied to select portions of the overall design and yield a pleasing range of yellow, orange, and brown highlights when fired. These color variations are as much a part of the overall design as the incised motifs they highlight.

At the same time he has pioneered the development of incised designs, Wilson has also refined his use of the appliqué technique. His appliqué work has become higher and higher in relief, and some of his best work is that of three-dimensional animals. Multispouted and/or multihandled jars, usually with spherical bodies and short necks, are among his favored vessel forms. One such jar entitled "Animals of the Four Sacred Mountains," featuring sculpted heads of a deer, buffalo, bear, and mountain sheep, was a prize winner at the 1985 Santa Fe Indian Market, where Wilson has been a consistent award winner since 1981.

Wilson has also won awards for his work at the Museum of Northern Arizona's Navajo Craftsman Exhibition, including a Best in Pottery award. Like Faye and Emmett Tso, he signs his work by incising his full name in block letters on the base of each vessel, along with the words "Navajo" and "Leupp, AZ." He has also taught his wife, Clara, to make pottery.

# CHAPTER 8

# REACHING BEYOND TRADITIONS

THE PREVIOUS CHAPTER discussed contemporary and innovative pitch-coated wares that are clearly linked to traditional Navajo pottery. Within the past fifteen years, however, several other Navajo potters have begun to produce painted and unpitched pottery that is less closely linked with the Navajo pottery tradition. In most cases, these wares reflect entirely new directions for Navajo pottery and are often more closely related to Pueblo pottery.

The number of Navajo potters who are forging these new avenues is very limited and it is difficult to make more than a few generalizations about their work. Collectively, their pottery shows an even greater degree of individuality and artistic creativity than that of any of the potters discussed in the previous chapter. Several of these potters use clay gathered on or near the Hopi Indian Reservation, because its purer texture provides a more suitable surface for painted designs and because it fires to a more aesthetically pleasing color. At least two of these very innovative potters learned their craft from Pueblo potters, and although all of them have developed personal designs and styles, the range of vessel forms also shows a strong Pueblo influence, as do the preparation and use of earth pigments. Nevertheless, the designs, themselves, are clearly rooted in Navajo culture.

84

For these pioneering artists, pottery making is a very personal thing, allowing them even greater artistic freedom than is enjoyed by the more traditional Navajo potters. Overall, their work has greater commercial appeal than the pitch-coated wares, but the use of certain symbols and motifs that are still considered sacred by many Navajos has met with the same resistance from their own people as was shown when yei-style rugs and commercial sandpaintings were first produced earlier in this century. Despite these additional barriers, however, these potters have remained resolute in their artistic decisions, and their work has gained increasing recognition among collectors. Let us look at them individually.

CHRISTINE NOFCHISSEY McHORSE was born in Morenci, Arizona, and grew up living away from the Navajo Reservation. Because she learned to make pottery from her husband's grandmother, Lena Archuleta, a well-known potter from Taos Pueblo, Christine's pottery is less Navajo in appearance than that of any of the other contemporary potters. Although she draws upon her own Navajo traditions, she finds inspiration in other cultures as well.

For her vessels, Christine chooses clay found near Taos. Because the clay is naturally rich in mica, no additional tempering material is required. Nevertheless, preparing the clay and allowing it to "cure" is a time-consuming process that requires several days. Vessels are built up using

*Chris McHorse, Santa Fe, New Mexico, 1986*

85

*Pot by Chris McHorse*

the traditional coiling technique and are then shaped into contemporary forms. Christine calls her style "free form," by which she means she starts with standardized shapes and then modifies them, exploring her own artistic feelings in the process. The rim of a vessel, for instance, is sometimes cut away to produce an asymmetrical shape, or it might be fashioned to resemble the steps on a ceremonial Pueblo kiva.

Decoration may include a few appliquéd motifs, but these are generally kept to a minimum; some vessels are simply burnished. Her intention is not to overpower the natural beauty of the clay, itself. In this regard, her pottery is not unlike that of Alice Cling's pitched wares.

Once a vessel is shaped, it is fired in an electric kiln. Previously, Christine fired her pottery outdoors using cottonwood bark as the fuel, but she now prefers a kiln because the temperatures are more consistent and easier to control. Also there is little chance of carbonization or fire-

86

*Pot by Chris McHorse*

clouding. Still, whenever someone requests that a piece be fired outdoors, she obliges them.

Christine has been an award winner at the Santa Fe Indian Market since 1983. Additional awards have been garnered at the New Mexico State Fair and at the Inter-Tribal Indian Ceremonial. She has also demonstrated her craft at the New Mexico State Fair and has had numerous shows at leading galleries and museums. In addition to being an accomplished potter, she is also an excellent silversmith.

LUCY LEUPP McKELVEY first learned to make pottery around 1973 as a college student, working with ceramic clays and firing them in an electric kiln. Since then, she has turned to the use of native clay collected near

*Lucy McKelvey at Santa Fe Indian Market, 1986*

Low Mountain, Arizona, which she mixes with sherd temper. Her elaborate geometric and lifeform designs are executed in natural pigments made from hematite, beeplant, and various clays. One of her most popular designs is that of yei figures, for which she prefers a large vessel such as a low squat jar with a very wide and flat shoulder. Once polished and painted, vessels are fired outside for up to six hours. Oak is the fuel used.

Lucy is a full-time elementary school teacher in Bluff, Utah, where she and her family reside. Despite her job, she still finds time to make pottery throughout the year to fill orders from dealers and private collectors. She has exhibited her work at the Santa Fe Indian Market since 1975 and has taught her three daughters, Cecelia, Celeste, and Celinda, as well as many of her students, to make pottery.

*"Masks of the Nightway,"* pot by Lucy McKelvey

*"Big Summer Thunders," pot by Lucy McKelvey*

It is Lucy's belief that pottery must, to some extent, go beyond traditions. When Navajos tell her that it is wrong to paint yei figures on her pots, she explains that her pottery is a very personal thing, and the decision of which designs to use must be hers alone.

*Ida Sahmie*
*Pine Springs, Arizona, 1986*

IDA SAHMIE began making pottery less than three years ago after learning from her mother-in-law, Priscilla Namingha, a noted Hopi potter from the village of Polacca. Ida still collects her clay from the Hopi Reservation and usually mixes it with a small amount of yellow clay so it fires to a light tan color. Each pot is coiled, scraped, and polished to a very smooth finish.

Using natural red and white earth pigments and black paint made from beeplant, Ida paints her pottery with a yucca brush. Yei figures and sand-painting motifs, such as that of Mother Earth and Father Sky, are her most frequently requested Navajo designs, but she has also done pieces with rug designs and wedding basket patterns. One of the most interesting pieces she has done to date is a hand-painted yei mask, decorated with feathers.

For a time, Ida and her husband, Louie, lived at Polacca on the Hopi Reservation, and it was there that she first developed a following for her

*Pot by Ida Sahmie (Navajo Tribal Museum collection)*

92

*Pottery mug by Ida Sahmie (Keams Canyon Arts and Crafts collection)*

pottery. Today they live near Ida's family in the Pine Springs area on the Navajo Reservation, where her work continues to attract widespread attention, bringing in more orders from collectors than she can immediately fill.

In 1986, Ida won a blue ribbon for a beautiful jar with a Mother Earth–Father Sky design at the Navajo Craftsman Exhibition at the Museum of Northern Arizona. Also in 1986, she won a first place award at the Navajo Nation Fair. She currently produces mostly small vessels measuring eight inches or smaller, but would like to try some larger works, despite having experienced the frustration of larger pieces breaking during the firing process. All of her vessels are fired outdoors using wood and manure as fuel.

Like Lucy McKelvey, Ida has also received some criticism from a few Navajos concerning her use of yei figures on her pottery, and for that reason, her family had a "sing" conducted for her to ward off any harm that might befall her. However, she too feels that her pottery is something very personal and sees no harm in painting yei designs on her work.

Blanche and Daniel Sales are from the Low Mountain, Arizona, area and learned to make pottery about twenty years ago from Daniel's grandfather. Although they also make the traditional pitch-coated pottery, they have been chosen for inclusion here because of their painted wares. Like several other potters discussed in this chapter, they utilize a Hopi clay found near their home. All of their pots are highly polished and fired outdoors, using manure as fuel.

Most of their pots are painted with geometric designs, including feathers, clouds, and thunderbirds. These are executed in a fine-lined style, using black or brown felt-tipped pens. Vessel forms include small and medium-sized jars and bowls and a variety of pipes. Blanche is a practicing herbalist, and thus much of her and her husband's more traditional, undecorated pottery is sold to Navajos; the decorated wares are usually bought by non-Navajos.

In addition to the painted wares, Daniel also decorates some of his work using the sgraffito technique, in which a design is carved on the surface of a pot after it has been fired. The resultant design appears in the col-

94

*Blanche and Daniel Sales*
*Low Mountain, Arizona,*
*1986*

*Pottery by Daniel and Blanche Sales (Navajo Tribal Museum collection* back row, right; and front row, center and right)

or of the underlying clay rather than in the color of the pot's surface. This technique has been popularized in recent years by a number of Rio Grande Pueblo potters, but Sales is the only Navajo to currently use it on hand-made pottery. Designs done in this technique include floral motifs and medallion-like designs, some of which have turquoise nuggets in their centers.

Both Blanche and Daniel Sales sign most of their pottery by printing their full names and the word "Navajo" in block letters on the base. Pipes, however, are never signed.

JOHN WHITEROCK was discussed in Chapter 7 for his pitch-coated pottery but is also included here because of his use of the sandpainting technique to decorate some of his pottery. His initial use of this technique in 1981 was limited to simple line geometrics, but he has more recently begun covering the entire surface of vessels with scenes of Navajo life, such as

95

96

*Sandpainted pot by John Whiterock (Collection of Jan Musial)*

John Whiterock
Cow Springs, Arizona, 1986

wedding or pastoral scenes, or very elaborate geometric patterns. His complex and very detailed designs usually require the use of many different colors.

John is one of only a few potters to use the sandpainting technique on handmade pottery. From a commercial standpoint, there is the major disadvantage in that once handmade pottery has been completely covered with a sandpainted design, it is sometimes difficult, although not impossible, to distinguish from slip-cast ceramic vessels that have been similarly decorated. These latter pieces are inexpensively produced for the curio market and can often be recognized on the basis of their very smooth interior surfaces. Handmade pottery, on the other hand, will usually be somewhat uneven on the interior surface.

Recently John has initialed some of his work in sand, but even this is unlikely to earn his work a higher price than the less expensive ceramic pieces. Still, John maintains that he gets a certain degree of personal satisfaction from making the pottery as well as decorating it.

# CHAPTER 9

# SUMMARY AND PREDICTIONS

REVITALIZATION in the field of Navajo pottery has been in process now for nearly thirty years. During that period, the number of Navajo women and men actively engaged in making pottery has increased, along with the quantity and quality of their work. For the first time, a real, albeit limited, market exists for Navajo pottery outside the Navajo culture.

The initial nurturing of this market and its continued vitality are the result of many factors, including the continued interest shown by certain key non-Navajo individuals, the collecting interests and strategies of several museums, the conservatism and continuity of Navajo ceremonialism and tradition, Navajo economics, and a changing public perception of and appreciation for Navajo pottery. Perhaps most important, however, is the creativity of individual Navajo potters in response to the commercial market, as shown in the works illustrated herein.

It is still difficult to predict exactly where the future of Navajo pottery will lead. Certainly the doomsday predictions made by anthropologists in the 1930s concerning the dying nature of Navajo pottery have been dispelled once and for all. Navajo pottery is not dying. Indeed, it is perhaps more alive today than ever before, not only in the sense of surviving but, more importantly, in the sense that its practitioners can explore and experiment with new ideas.

Responding to commercialism during the past few decades, especially during the last decade, Navajo potters have tried out new vessel forms that, in some cases, have differed radically from the jars and bowls previously being made for traditional Navajo use, which had changed little during the past century. Many of these new forms have clearly been suggested by Pueblo examples, while others, such as whimsical banks and other effigy forms, show more individual creativity. Modeled three-dimensional animal figures have a long tradition in Navajo culture as unfired mud toys, but similar figures were not fired and coated with pitch until the 1960s.

The 1960s and 1970s witnessed a virtual explosion in the variety of appliquéd designs appearing on Navajo pottery, the most popular being animal and plant motifs. These have been copied over and over by many of today's Navajo potters, making it almost impossible to determine with any real certainty who first used some of the most common motifs presently in use.

Despite this sometimes overindulgent tendency among Navajo potters to copy one another's designs, either directly or indirectly, the past twenty years have brought several potters to the forefront of the current market. These individuals have developed unique styles that are readily identifiable whether their work is signed or not. The names of Silas Claw, Alice Cling, Faye Tso, and Jimmy Wilson are synonymous with delicately sculpted and appliquéd plant and animal motifs, highly polished vessels with minimal decoration, large appliquéd designs, and ornate incised geometric designs, respectively. Similarly, the work of nearly every other potter discussed in this book can be identified by the practiced eye on the basis of vessel form and treatment of certain decorative elements.

Because pottery making is an art form, experimentation is a key operative and can be expected to remain so in future years. Even those potters who have developed very personal styles and designs have done so over a period of years, and it has been interesting to watch these styles evolve. To a large extent, however, experimentation, too, is guided and controlled by the market. Innovations that are not accepted by the buying public are quickly discontinued, whereas those that are accepted are further developed, leading to still other innovations. Jimmy Wilson's early designs, for example, were very simple, shallow incised motifs drawn on the surface of a pot. These gradually became bolder and more deeply incised. Next he began to arrange his designs within banded zones, and most

*Pottery figurines (Navajo Tribal Museum collection)*

recently, these bands have been accentuated through the use of clay-slip paints of various colors.

Such experimentation was all but impossible in the absence of a commercial market and when potters were bound by ceremonial and/or psychological restrictions. Today, however, few, if any, limitations are placed upon a potter's creativity. Increasing emphasis on overall quality is certainly to be expected in the future as potters learn that more careful attention to symmetry, surface polishing, and an even application of the pitch will command higher prices for their work.

This is not to say that in the future Navajo pottery will only be produced for a commercial market. The pottery tradition is too deeply rooted in Navajo culture to allow that to happen. The need for Navajo pottery in a ceremonial context will never die, and although many of today's potters make pottery both for traditional Navajo needs as well as for the tourist market, such may not always be the case. In the future, it is likely that the less traditional and/or more creative potters will cater increasingly to the collectors' market, whereas Navajo needs might be served by individuals who have been raised more traditionally.

Based on the author's interviews with Navajo potters, the future is also likely to witness a continuing increase in their numbers. Most of the potters discussed herein have taught their children or other relatives how to make pottery, and with the market for Navajo pottery still in its infancy, public demand for the product is certain to increase. Too, current interest among tribal leaders in tourism development and promotion can only spur the growth of existing markets for native crafts.

Vessels with animal and other life forms decorating them have proven to be among the most popular to date. Increasing realism in the depiction of animals and plants, whether as appliquéd motifs or as fully sculpted three-dimensional figurines, can be expected. Figurines of domestic and exotic animals have long been in production, and a number of potters have already sculpted animals in action poses. Both Faye Tso and Silas Claw have made human figures, and Silas has even grouped together figures of people and animals in a rodeo scene. An expected development would be the production of nativities, already a popular trend among Pueblo potters.

For those potters who are expressing themselves in both painted and unpainted wares that are clearly outside the tradition of pitch-coated pottery and intended primarily for collectors, the market is even more unlimited. Because the production of finely painted pottery by Navajos is such a recent phenomenon, these potters have the luxury of defining their own boundaries. As evidenced by the interest shown in their work at the Santa Fe Indian Market and by the willingness of leading art galleries to feature their work, these potters have thus far only begun to tap the market.

Navajo pottery has never held wide appeal to those who collect southwestern Indian pottery, but as potters continue to improve the quality of their work and demonstrate increased variety and creativity, public demand is sure to increase. Because of the strong market already established for painted Pueblo pottery, the contemporary painted Navajo wares have a greater potential to capture a share of the collectors' market, but the pitched wares are also gaining increasing acceptance and can now be found in leading galleries in Santa Fe, Albuquerque, Phoenix, and other major cities, as well as in the gift shops of leading museums.

What will the economic effect be from all this? To be certain, the price of Navajo pottery has risen steadily within the past few years, especially for works by the more established potters. Overall, Navajo pitched pottery is still very inexpensive in comparison with Pueblo pottery, but individual pieces selling for several hundred dollars are not uncommon. In the field of the newer painted varieties of Navajo pottery, larger works by

Lucy McKelvey and Christine McHorse frequently command prices in excess of $1,000, making them comparable, and rightly so, with works by leading Pueblo potters. Overall, Navajo pottery may never command the widespread appeal afforded Pueblo pottery, but for the discriminating and astute collector, works by today's leading Navajo potters could indeed prove to be an excellent investment.

# REFERENCES

Amsden, Charles A. [1934]. *Navaho weaving: Its technic and history.* Reprint. Glorieta, New Mexico: Rio Grande Press.

Bailey, Lynn R. 1970. *Bosque Redondo: An American concentration camp.* Pasadena: Socio-Technical Books.

Beaver, William T. 1952. Navaho pottery and basketry. *Masterkey* 26(3):109.

_____. Personal communication to author. Flagstaff, Arizona. 20 June 1986.

Bell, Jan. 1982. Some observations on the museum as agent of change. *Council for Museum Anthropology Newsletter* 6(4):9–14.

Brugge, David M. 1964. Navajo ceramic practices. *Southwestern Lore* 30(3):37–46.

_____. 1968. *Navajos in the Catholic Church records of New Mexico, 1694–1875.* Research Report 1. Window Rock, Arizona: Navajo Tribe, Parks and Recreation Research Section.

_____. 1981. *Navajo pottery and ethnohistory.* Revised edition. Navajo Nation Papers in Anthropology 4. Window Rock, Arizona: Navajo Nation Cultural Resource Management Program. (Originally published in 1963 as Navajoland Publications, Series 2. Window Rock, Arizona: Navajo Tribal Museum).

_____. 1983. Navajo history and prehistory to 1850. In *Southwest.* Vol. 10 of *Handbook of North American Indians,* ed. by Alfonso Ortiz. Washington, D. C.: Smithsonian Institution.

————, and J. Lee Correll. 1970. *The story of the Navajo treaties*. Navajoland Historical Publications, Documentary Series 1. Window Rock, Arizona: Navajo Tribe, Parks and Recreation Research Section.

Carlson, Roy L. 1965. *Eighteenth century Navajo fortresses of the Gobernador District; the Earl Morris Papers, 2*. University of Colorado Studies in Anthropology 10. Boulder, Colorado: University of Colorado Press.

Cella, Nancy S., Gary O. Rollefson, and Alan H. Simmons. 1984. Prehistoric site descriptions. In *Archaeological investigations in the Gallegos Canyon area; Blocks IV and V of the NIIP*, assembled by William E. Reynolds, Nancy S. Cella, and Evelyn J. Caballero. Albuquerque: Chambers Consultants and Planners.

Dittert, Alfred E. Jr. 1958. *Preliminary archaeological investigations in the Navajo project area of northwestern New Mexico*. Museum of New Mexico Papers in Anthropology, Navajo Project Series 1.

————, James J. Hester, and Frank W. Eddy. 1961. *An archaeological survey of the Navajo Reservoir District, northwestern New Mexico*. Monographs of the School of American Research and the Museum of New Mexico 23.

Douglas, Frederic H. 1937. *Seven Navajo pots*. Material Culture Notes 3. Denver: Denver Art Museum.

Farmer, Malcolm F. 1942. Navaho archaeology of Upper Blanco and Largo canyons, northwestern New Mexico. *American Antiquity* 8(1):65–79.

Forbes, Jack D. 1960. *Apache, Navaho and Spaniard*. Norman: University of Oklahoma Press.

Haile, Berard. 1938. *Origin legend of the Navajo Enemy Way*. Yale University Publications in Anthropology 17. New Haven, Conn.: Yale University Press.

Hill, W. W. 1937. *Navajo pottery manufacture*. University of New Mexico Bulletin, Anthropological Series 2(3):1–23.

Hurt, Wesley. 1942. Eighteenth century Navajo hogans from Canyon de Chelly National Monument. *American Antiquity* 8:89–104.

James, Marjorie. 1937. A note on Navajo pottery making. *El Palacio* 43, nos. 13–15.

Kidder, A. V. 1922. Ruins of the historic period in the upper San Juan Valley, New Mexico. *American Anthropologist* 22:322–29.

Maxwell, Gilbert S. 1963. *Navajo rugs: Past, present & future.* Palm Desert, Calif.: Best-West Publications.

McGreevey, Susan Brown. 1982. Woven holy people: Navajo sandpainting textiles. In *Woven Holy People: Navajo Sandpainting Textiles.* Santa Fe: Wheelwright Museum of the American Indian.

Matthews, Washington. 1897. Navaho legends. *Memoirs of the American Folklore Society* 5. Boston: Houghton, Mifflin and Company.

Parezo, Nancy J. 1983. *Navajo sandpainting; from religious act to commercial art.* Tucson: University of Arizona Press.

————. 1986. Now is the time to collect. *Masterkey* 59(4):11–18.

Reeve, Frank D. 1960. Navajo Spanish diplomacy, 1770–1790. *New Mexico Historical Review* 35(3):200–35.

Roessel, Robert. 1982. *Navajo arts and crafts.* Rough Rock, Arizona: Navajo Curriculum Center.

Roessel, Ruth, and Broderick H. Johnson (comp.). 1974. *Navajo livestock reduction: A national disgrace.* Tsaile, Arizona: Navajo Community College Press.

Russell, Scott C. 1981. Recent developments in Navajo pottery. Paper presented at meeting, Issues and Images: New Dimensions in Native American Art History. Tempe, Arizona: Arizona State University. April.

————, and Mark B. McDonald. 1982. The economic contributions of women in a rural western Navajo community. *American Indian Quarterly* 6(3–4):262–82.

Sapir, Edward, and Albert G. Sandoval. 1930. A note on Navajo pottery making. *American Anthropologist* 32(3):575–76.

Schroeder, Albert H. 1965. A brief history of the southern Utes. *Southwestern Lore* 30(4):53–78.

Stephen, A. M. 1893. The Navajo. *American Anthropologist* 6(4):345–62.

Thompson, Gerald E. 1976. *The army and the Navajo: The Bosque Redondo reservation experiment.* Tucson: University of Arizona Press.

Tschopik, Harry Jr. 1938. Taboo as a possible factor involved in the obsolescence of Navaho pottery and basketry. *American Anthropologist* 40(2):257–62.

———. 1941. *Navaho pottery making; an inquiry into the affinities of Navaho painted pottery.* Papers of the Peabody Museum of Archaeology and Ethnology 17(1).

U.S. Congress. 1937. *Survey of conditions of the Indians in the United States.* Hearings before a Subcommittee of the Senate Committee on Indian Affairs, 75th Congress, Part 34. Washington, D.C.: U.S. Government Printing Office.

Wright, H. Diane. 1980. Navajo pottery wins new appreciation. *The Indian Trader* (April): 31,44,47.

Wyman, Leland. 1970. *Blessingway.* Tucson: University of Arizona Press.

# INDEX

Medicine men: influence on potters, 39, 40; use of pottery by, 40
Modeling: *See* Decorating
Mother Earth, Father Sky: 91, 93
Museum of Northern Arizona: 47, 49. *See also* Navajo Craftsman Exhibition

Namingha, Priscilla: 91
Navajo Craftsman Exhibition: 43, 47, 62, 74, 77, 83, 93
Navajo Gray pottery: 30, 33-35
Navajo Indians: population of, 3; location of reservation, 3; early history of, 3-7; adoption of puebloan traits, 4-5; current conditions of, 8; Navajo Tribal Council, 7, 8
Navajo Nation Fair: 66, 79, 93
Navajo Painted pottery: 33
Navajo Polychrome pottery: 33
Navajo Tribal Council: *See* Navajo Indians
Navajo Tribal Museum: 49
New Mexico State Fair: 66, 87

Painting: Navajo tradition against, 23; revival of, 23; use of acrylic and enamel paints, 26, 57, 58, 71
Pigments: 23, 88, 91
Piñon pitch: use of on pottery: 15, 25, 26, 54, 56, 58, 59, 62, 66, 80
Pinyon Gray pottery: 30, 35
Pipes: 14, 40, 80
Polishing: 19, 62
Polishing stones: *See* tools
Pottery: origins of among Navajo, 9; cultural significance of, 9-11, 28; utilitarian use of, 11-12; *See also* Ceremonialism
Price: *See* Marketing

Sahmie, Ida: 91, 93-94
Sales, Blanche: 94-95
Sales, Daniel: 94-95
Sand: *See* Temper
Sandpainting: commercial development of, 26, 45-46; use on pottery, 26, 77, 95, 97